FIRESIDE

SIMON &
SCHUSTER

SIMON & SCHUSTER'S

Two-Minute Crosswords

SERIES 1

David King

A FIRESIDE BOOK
Published by Simon & Schuster Inc.
New York   London   Toronto   Sydney   Tokyo   Singapore

FIRESIDE
Rockefeller Center
1230 Avenue of the Americas
New York, New York 10020

FIRESIDE and colophon
are registered trademarks of Simon & Schuster Inc.

Designed by The Bedford Book Works Inc.

Manufactured in the United States of America

10 9 8 7 6 5 4 3 2 1

ISBN: 0-671-88574-X

For Peg

Every reason I care about love:
breathless, endless, reckless, true.

ACKNOWLEDGMENT

Thanks to Joel Fishman
for the idea, the sale, and the contract.

FOREWORD

Welcome to an exciting new puzzle series! The crosswords in this book are unique—small enough to be finished in minutes, yet so addictive you'll find it hard to solve just one. Don't let the size fool you, though. Their combination of clever clues and wonderful words will give your wits a first-rate workout.

The puzzles start out easy, then get tougher. By the time you've made it through the final Ferocious Five, you'll agree: Miniatures are marvelous! Be sure to keep your eyes open for Simon & Schuster's Two-Minute Crosswords Series #2, coming soon to stores near you. With your support, there'll be many more collections to come. Please send your comments and suggestions to:

David King
Fireside Books
1230 Avenue of the Americas
New York, NY 10020

SIMON & SCHUSTER'S

Two-Minute Crosswords

ACROSS

1 Employees
6 Shed tears
9 The Pied ___
10 "Yes," in voting
11 Abundant
12 Church bench
13 Sort of desk
15 Leg joint
16 "If the shoe ___, . . ."
19 Passage across
21 Jelly holder
23 Slightly crazy
24 Be in debt
25 Ring-shaped island
26 Hive dweller
27 Noisy fight

DOWN

1 Brief flash of light
2 Shakespeare's "___ of Athens"
3 It bears fruit
4 Hall of Fame pitcher
5 Be worried
6 Youngster's gun
7 Ham on ___
8 Kind of evergreen
14 Important
17 Book's name
18 Fashionableness
20 "Batman" actor West
21 Task
22 Supernatural dread

PUZZLE 2

ACROSS

1 Confusing collection of rooms and passages
5 Large tree branch
9 Beasts of burden
10 Singer Adams
11 Tendency
12 Cab
13 Former TV host Sullivan
15 Egg layer
16 Swedish tennis player
20 Scientist's workplace
21 Gangster Capone
22 Oil cartel: abbr.
24 Salt Lake City's state
28 Get money for a check
29 Large book
30 Pants patch place
31 Semiprecious stone

DOWN

1 Disorderly crowd
2 Lumberjack's tool
3 Variety of Buddhism
4 Go in
5 Allow
6 Where Boise is
7 Kitchen appliance
8 For the time ___
14 Genetic substance: abbr.
16 Child's toy brick
17 Asian nation
18 Overweight
19 Popeye's foe
23 Guerrilla Guevara
25 2,000 pounds
26 Etiquette expert Vanderbilt
27 Evil spell

PUZZLE 3

ACROSS

1 Parakeet's cry
6 Barely-hit ball
8 Do damage to
9 "Planet of the ___"
11 Large boats
12 Made a loan
13 Note after "do"
14 Negative reply
15 Agreement
18 Not quite closed
20 City in Norway
21 Act out
22 Baby frog
24 Somewhat wet

DOWN

1 Kind of oak bark
2 Sings through closed lips
3 Letter before em
4 And others: abbr.
5 It can be smoked
6 China, Japan, etc.
7 Writer's alias
8 Groucho's brother
10 Place to shop
16 Seafood with a shell
17 Commotion
18 Biblical prophet
19 Leave at the altar
23 Greek letter

PUZZLE 4

ACROSS

1 Certain
5 Japanese mountain
9 Use one's teeth
10 Not near
11 Govern
12 Wine-bottle stopper
13 Pitcher's stat: abbr.
14 That man
15 Madame Tussaud's place
20 "You said ___!"
21 Cell material: Abbr.
22 Economist Karl
25 Footwear
26 Baseball's Matty
27 Not working
28 Opposite of shallow
29 Look closely

DOWN

1 Tighten a lid
2 "Star Trek" lieutenant
3 Get less tense
4 Female sheep
5 Meets in person
6 Flying saucer, e.g.
7 Kitchen container
8 Irritate
14 Primitive grass house
16 Confusion
17 Wear away slowly
18 Mother's brother
19 One who creates
22 Angry
23 Alcoholic beverage
24 Fish eggs
25 Use a straw to drink

ACROSS

1 One plus one
4 ___ plug (car item)
9 Was in charge of
10 Song from the past
11 Piece of a play
12 Covered with wet dirt
13 Rink user
15 Praise too much
16 On the ocean
20 Sherlock of fiction
22 Direction reversal
25 Bug a bit
26 Message of a story
27 Father's Day gift
28 One-tenth of a dime
29 Wield an axe

DOWN

1 Worthless stuff
2 Eccentric
3 Available
4 "___ Like It Hot"
5 Opposite of singular
6 Sum up
7 Get ___ of
8 It opens a lock
14 Iran's capital
17 Common last name
18 Disturbingly weird
19 Crooked
21 "You ___ live once"
22 Baseball official, for short
23 Foot part
24 Large coffee container

ACROSS

1 Border on
5 Poses a question
9 Nonsense
10 Break with a sharp crack
11 Make an effort
13 Orangutan, for one
14 Kid's shooter
16 "Casey ___ the Bat"
18 ___ Paulo
19 Football score: abbr.
20 Movie schoolmaster
23 Be sick
24 Hand part
27 Con game
29 Opera song
30 Isle off Scotland
31 Words in a book

DOWN

1 "Honest ___"
2 Fight like Rocky
3 Secondhand
4 Beat badly
5 "___ the World Turns"
6 Unexpected difficulty
7 Ruined
8 Pay out, as money
12 Distinguishing quality
15 Formal headgear
16 Pile up
17 "___ or treat!"
21 Potter's material
22 Absolutely positive
25 Blend together
26 Animal Dracula becomes
28 "Are you talking to ___?"

ACROSS

1 Despise
5 "They were ___ for each other"
9 Syrian, e.g.
10 "Jeopardy!" host Trebek
11 Go under water with air tanks
13 Actress Eva
14 Gum flavor
18 Long-necked bird
19 "Last one in's a ___!"
24 Friends, in French
25 Out of whack
26 Small horse
27 Hair-salon wave

DOWN

1 Is owner of
2 Rainbow's shape
3 Greek letter
4 Go out, like the tide
5 Polite term for a lady
6 Excuse
7 English county
8 Put into use
12 See eye to eye
14 Throw on the junk heap
15 Ad
16 Kind of kitchen
17 Nervous
20 Snooze
21 Lamb's mom
22 Surly sound
23 Place to play basketball

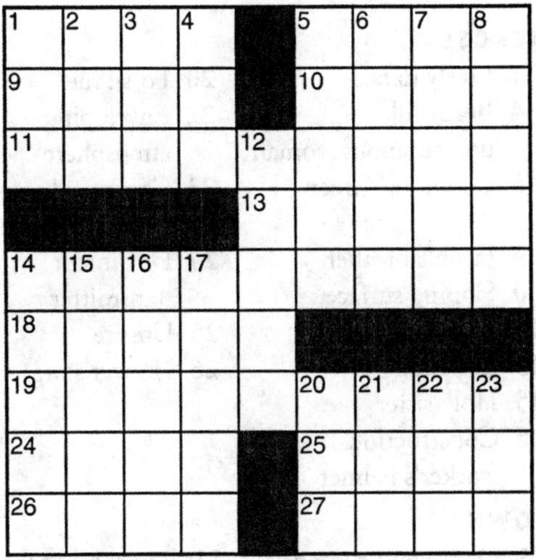

ACROSS

1 Lively dance
4 Beautiful, unscrupulous woman
8 Gabor of "Green Acres"
9 Jacob's brother
10 Sloping surface
12 Spellbound
13 Leg part
15 Holy sister
16 Construction worker's helmet
20 Fossil fuel
22 Enveloping atmosphere
23 Command to stop a march
24 Document transmitter
25 Unsure
26 Hoover's org.

DOWN

1 Obnoxious person
2 ___ the Terrible
3 Chess or checkers
4 Roofed porch
5 Without delay: Abbr.
6 Glove-compartment item
7 Stay ___ (remain in place)
11 Punishment for rule-breaking
14 Mutt
16 Fifty percent
17 ___ and puff
18 Man from Oman
19 Roll down a runway
20 Ho ___ Minh
21 Blockhead

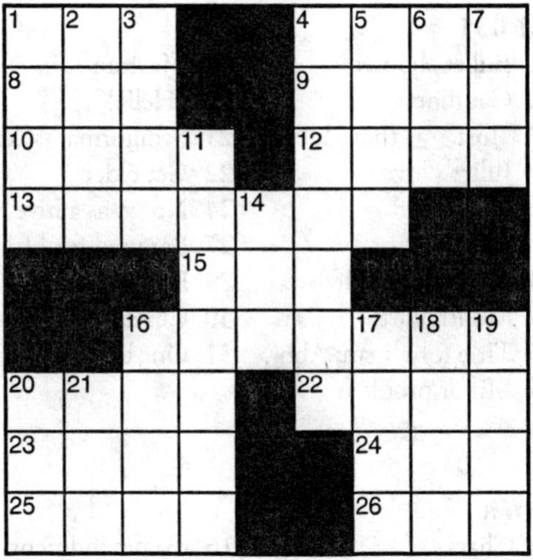

ACROSS

1 Bullet shooter
4 Gaudiness
9 "Just ___ thought!"
10 Juliet's love
11 Strummed instrument
13 Average, in golf
14 Mouth part
15 Title for a man: Abbr.
16 Minor problem
18 Mexican coin
20 "Hello!"
21 Semiformal jacket
22 Get older
24 Noisy, as a hive
27 Bar used for lifting
29 Female deer
30 Charlie Chaplin role
31 One billion years

DOWN

1 Chat
2 Springsteen's "Born in the ___"
3 Teenage Mutant ___ Turtles
4 Get bigger
5 "Behold!"
6 Little devil
7 Celtics and Red Sox
8 Superb swordsman
12 Drinking spree
16 Commandment word
17 African country
18 Bar, in Britain
19 Give off
21 Ball field protector
23 Actress ___ Marie Saint
25 Place to see pandas
26 Meditation discipline
28 Letter after el

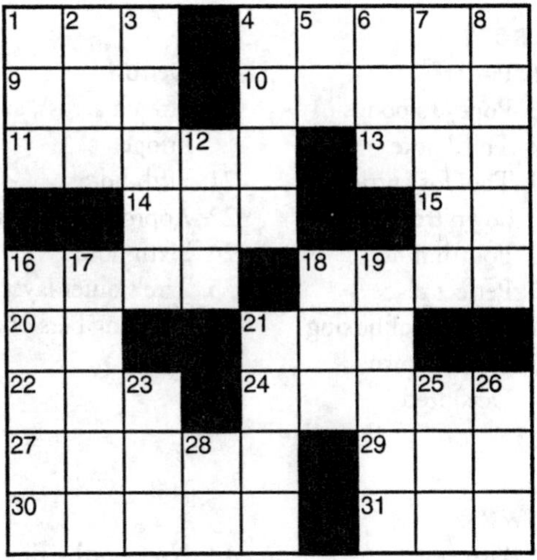
1
2
3
4
5
6
7
8
9
10
11
12
13
14
15
16
17
18
19
20
21
22
23
24
25
26
27
28
29
30
31

ACROSS

1 Put off
6 Popeye's poopsie
7 Third note
9 Tool for cutting down trees
10 Fourth note
12 Perfect place
14 Do a bit of boxing
16 Piece of corn
17 Devoured
18 Defrost
20 Stretch across, as a bridge
21 Fifth note
22 Appropriate or fitting
24 Sixth note
25 Tire's outer layer
27 Opening bars of a song

DOWN

1 First note
2 Spirited self-assurance
3 Repair
4 Nights before holidays
5 Second note
7 Runs into
8 Boise's state
10 Death-causing
11 Large public show-place
13 Noteworthy time
15 Soft food for babies
19 Tell of a danger
20 "When You Wish Upon a ___"
23 Caress a cat
25 Seventh note
26 Eighth note

ACROSS

1 Run off to marry
6 Light-switch position
9 Sheets and pillow-cases
10 In favor of
11 "This ___ a stickup!"
12 Spinach gives him strength
14 Snoring, in comics
16 It rises each morning
17 Electron's home
19 Tulip, when planted
22 Month after April
24 "That's ___ for the course"
25 Car wheel cover
28 Yes, in Spain
29 "___ Had a Hammer"
30 High-IQ society
32 Edgar Allan ___
33 Fall in a faint

DOWN

1 ___ Doolittle ("My Fair Lady" role)
2 Composer Franz
3 "___ Top of Old Smokey"
4 Liveliness
5 Biblical old-timer
6 Become less inhibited
7 One way to cook eggs
8 Enemy
13 Alehouse
15 Undead creature
18 Popular computer, for short
20 Cowboy's rope
21 Director De Palma
23 Yellow vegetables
25 "With it"
26 ET's vehicle
27 Praying place
31 "Uh uh"

PUZZLE 12

ACROSS

1 Commercials
4 Highest card, often
7 Go bad
8 Weeding tool
9 People balance it
13 Bowling lane
14 Get on a horse
15 Cover a hole
16 Woman's shoe projection

20 Balloon-bursting sound
21 "___ drop of golden sun"
22 In ___ of (overwhelmed by)
23 "A Nightmare on ___ Street"

DOWN

1 Part of a circle
2 Play-___ (kid's material)
3 Heating system component
4 Naval greeting
5 Pigeon sound
6 Scream of fear
10 Loose outer garment
11 1971 Fonda / Sutherland film

12 Where baseball players sit
16 Fancy resort
17 Sound of a comic-book punch
18 Snake in the water
19 On the ___ (fleeing the law)

PUZZLE 13

ACROSS

1 It contains a variety of things
8 Let out of prison
9 Pertaining to birds
10 Make a run for it
13 Changes direction suddenly
14 Atlanta's state: Abbr.
15 Buildings for lodging
16 Guitarist Atkins
18 "Et ___, Brute!"
19 He sold his soul
20 Not no
22 Talk-show host Winfrey
23 Charles Dickens villain
25 Still

DOWN

1 Force that holds us on the earth
2 What the "R" in "I.R.S." means
3 Sci-fi/horror film
4 Grizzlies, for example
5 Forbids
6 Red ___ a beet
7 Hair conditioner, often
11 Way in the past
12 Gospel writer
16 Cooking chicken
17 One of the Great Lakes
19 Golfer's warning cry
21 Opposite of NNW
24 105 in Roman numerals

PUZZLE 14

ACROSS

1 Cola cooler
4 Senator Kennedy
7 Female horse
9 Guthrie of music
10 Evening hours, on TV
12 Stringed instrument
13 "Norma ___" (Sally Field movie)
14 The devil
16 Frontiersman planter Johnny
20 Null and ___
21 Actress Garr
22 Appropriate
23 What a beaver builds

DOWN

1 Small demon
2 Automobile
3 Norse explorer ___ the Red
4 Group of three
5 Tall tree
6 Deer's dear
8 Green gem
9 Minimally
11 Bring joy to
14 Barbecue rod
15 Requirement
16 Gardner of Hollywood
17 Dr. Seuss's "Hop on ___"
18 Important period
19 Somewhat dark

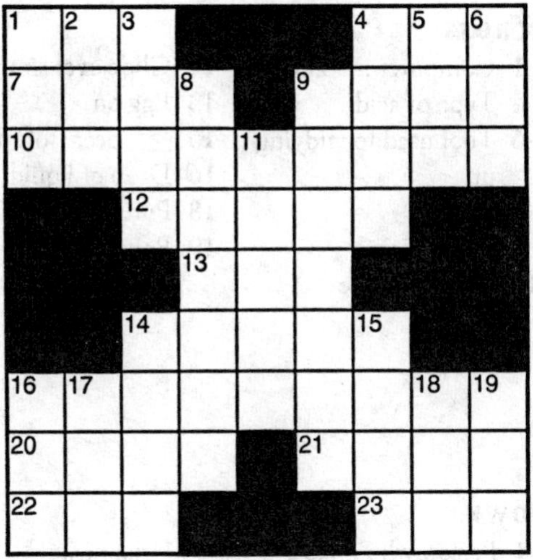
1
2
3
4
5
6
7
8
9
10
11
12
13
14
15
16
17
18
19
20
21
22
23

ACROSS

1 Computer in "2001"
4 Type of acid
6 Tool used for tidying up
8 Weight
9 Once again
11 On's opposite
12 Glide over snow
13 Egg on
15 ___ beer (soft drink)
16 Drop of liquid
18 Pure, fresh air
19 Ram's mate

DOWN

1 Person who gives a party
2 Museum material
3 Peru's capital
4 ". . . where the ___ roam . . ."
5 Make feel less sad
6 Clear moisture from a car window
7 Indian tea
8 Adult swine
10 Quick sense of humor
14 Take a light nap
15 Ancient alphabetic character
17 Archer's weapon

ACROSS

1 Freud subject
4 Tip of an antler
6 Cute cartoon characters
10 Yes, in French
11 "___ a Yellow Ribbon . . ."
12 Verb modifier: Abbr.
13 Adam's partner
14 Agent's org.
15 "Slippery when ___"
16 Unwanted, troubling problem
20 Quarterback John
21 But then again. . .

DOWN

1 Before, old-style
2 Hunk of gunk
3 "___ at a time"
4 Army's lowest rank
5 Entrance in a wall
6 Team leader
7 Of sound
8 Metal fastener
9 Take care of
17 Single layer
18 Have a debt with
19 Tit for ___

PUZZLE 17

ACROSS

1 Forehead
5 Mite of matter
9 Wife of Jacob
10 Still-life subject
11 Disassemble
13 "A Man For ___ Seasons"
14 ___ the line (follow orders closely)
15 Belly
16 Straight, hard hit in baseball
22 Stench
23 Divisible by two
24 Bait for a fishhook
25 Looked at

DOWN

1 Common sandwich: abbr.
2 "The Crying Game" actor
3 Furniture wood
4 Bread enricher
5 Fruit provider
6 "___ For Two"
7 Rower's need
8 Actor who wears lots of chains
12 Audibly
16 Opposite of high
17 Wedding words
18 It goes with "neither"
19 College vine
20 Letter before double-you
21 Put a stop to

PUZZLE 18

ACROSS

1 Antlered animal
4 Door-frame piece
8 Seethe with rage
10 Kind of code
11 Costello's partner in humor
13 "___ Fair Lady"
14 One of the Three Stooges
15 Be idle
18 Neighbor of Burma
19 Inspire wonder in
20 "You Are ___ Beautiful"
21 Fairy's purchase?
26 Gumbo vegetable
27 "Not guilty," e.g.
28 Get what one's sown
29 "That'll be the ___!"

DOWN

1 Flow out
2 Hall-of-Famer Gehrig
3 Billy the ___
4 Boxer's blow
5 Smell
6 "Same here"
7 Norman in "Psycho"
9 Flimsy, as an excuse
12 "One if ___ land. . ."
15 Work
16 Not sleeping
17 Striped animal
18 Fancy airplane maneuver
20 "___ Elsewhere"
22 Jabber
23 Getting on in years
24 Coffee alternative
25 Dried grass

ACROSS

1 Indonesian island
5 Poke
8 The yokes on them
9 "Oh, what's the ___?"
10 Preaching passage
11 Buck's mate
12 Let go from a job
15 Flock member
16 Lock, stock and ___
19 Feminist cause: abbr.
20 Minnelli of movies
24 ___ and vigor
25 What the nose knows
26 Canine comment
27 Canine comment

DOWN

1 Make a quick note
2 Tin Man's tool
3 Peeve
4 Deer's head growth
5 Form of self-defense
6 Since
7 Meat from cows
13 Reverence + fear + wonder
14 "Follow the ___ brick road"
16 Group of girls
17 What a diva delivers
18 Parking garage feature
21 Answer to "Who wants ice cream?"
22 Wild animal collection
23 Canine comment

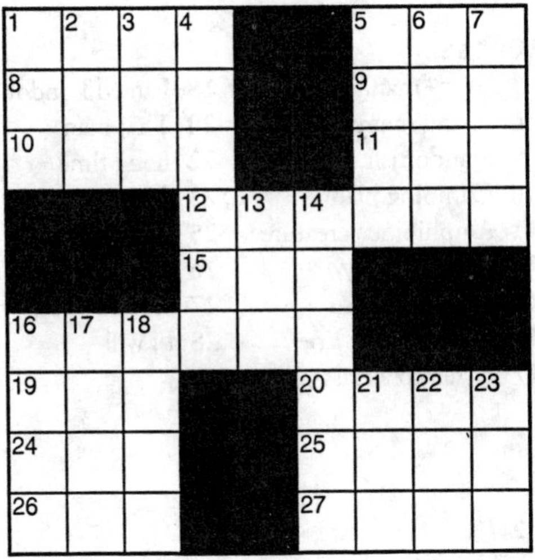
1
2
3
4
5
6
7
8
9
10
11
12
13
14
15
16
17
18
19
20
21
22
23
24
25
26
27

PUZZLE 20

ACROSS

1 Very "manly"
6 Flying mammal
9 Standoffish
10 Climbing plant
11 Amphibious creature
12 Move quickly
13 Former spouse
14 City on Lake Erie
17 Listen to a class
18 Famed London bell
20 That man
22 Long time
23 Badness
25 Ram's mate
26 Oddity
27 Handle roughly
28 Ill will

DOWN

1 Horse's neck hair
2 Writer Haley
3 Mooing animal
4 Soaking spot
5 "___ course!"
   (certainly)
6 "Carmen" composer
7 Enthusiastic
8 Secretary's error
15 Kind of poem
16 Place to see a suspect
17 Nixon's VP
18 Honk a horn
19 Sioux City state
20 Jazz trumpeter Al
21 Actress Sommer
24 Seven, on a sundial
26 "Mind your P's
   and ___"

PUZZLE 21

ACROSS

1 Caustic substance
5 Flower stalk
9 Tarzan's mate
10 Smoky air
11 Actress Bancroft
12 Paid performer, familiarly
13 Do, ___, mi, . . .
14 Puzzle type
17 Expert
18 Twain's Tom
21 Via
23 ___ Jima
24 Soft cheese
26 Countdown ending
28 Greek letter
29 Bible garden
30 Lustful look

DOWN

1 Open a bit
2 Walker's aid
3 Lodging provider
4 Record player
5 "Quiet!"
6 Bugle call
7 Poet Pound
8 Cat cry
15 Cover a cake
16 Child's pet
18 Extent
19 Full of wonder
20 Had on
21 Light snack
22 Twelve months
25 Fish eggs
27 Atop

PUZZLE 22

ACROSS

1 Colorful parrot
6 ___ the beaten path
9 Radiate
10 Ghost's shout
11 229-year-old TV character
12 Actress Collins
13 Where Ted Williams played
16 ". . . and justice for ___"
17 "My, my!"
23 Cincinnati's state
24 It's used to chop wood
25 Competed in a race
26 Capital of France
28 Manager's degree: Abbr.
29 "___ is as good as a mile"

DOWN

1 Lunch or supper
2 It joins two wheels
3 Fold at the end of a sleeve
4 Message from the sponsor
5 "The Way ___ Were"
6 Double-reed instrument
7 Young horse
8 Doting
12 Leave high and dry
14 Mexican menu item
15 Soar through the air
17 Outer shape
18 Skipper in "Moby Dick"
19 One of Columbus's boats
20 Spy Mata ___
21 Allies' adversaries
22 "___ of the D'Urbervilles"
26 Dad
27 "I think, therefore I ___"

1	2	3	4	5		6	7	8
9						10		
11					12			
13			14	15				
			16					
17	18	19				20	21	22
23						24		
25				26	27			
28				29				

ACROSS

1 Walks, in baseball: abbr.
4 Play a part in a play
7 Swiss peak
8 Reef material
11 Basic rule
13 Rose or Incaviglia of baseball
14 Dorothy's dog
15 A shot ___ the dark
16 China's Chou ___-lai
17 Vertical fence piece
20 Actress Miles
22 Moving stairs
24 Sordid or squalid
25 Cape in Massachusetts
26 Golf ball holder
27 Medical insurance plan: Abbr.

DOWN

1 Scottish instrument
2 Busybody
3 Roasting rod
4 It often beats a king
5 Young male horse
6 Group of three musicians
9 Place to sit and wait
10 ___ da Vinci
12 Nom ___ plume
18 "Go away, cat!"
19 Not wild
20 Norfolk's state: Abbr.
21 Draw with acid
23 Soap ingredient

PUZZLE 24

ACROSS

1 Item food is served on
5 Pal
9 "___ upon a time. . ."
10 Nevada city
11 Common sweetener
13 Rap on a door
14 "Better you than ___"
15 Dashboard button
18 Contented sigh
20 Flat container for liquor
23 "Well, I'll be!"
26 Largest continent
27 Short business note
28 "Better luck ___ time"
29 Front of a ship

DOWN

1 Landing pier
2 Privy to
3 Food fish
4 As a result
5 Weep
6 Belonging to that woman
7 E pluribus ___
8 Act dull and dispirited
12 Small, light, open boat
16 Gripping appliance
17 Enthusiastic
18 Strong ___ ox
19 Firetruck equipment
21 Heavyweight wrestling
22 Be aware of
24 Veto
25 Kind of bran

PUZZLE 25

ACROSS

1 Member of a Mexican empire
6 Breach
9 African river
10 Tax-deferred investment vehicle: Abbr.
11 Excited by
12 Spirited dance
13 13th letter
14 Residence
16 Blender setting

18 Change to fit better
20 Unit of weight: Abbr.
22 Great pleasure
23 Calcutta's country
26 Rented set of rooms: Abbr.
27 Dr. ___ (children's author)
28 Race a car's engine
29 Twist and pinch

DOWN

1 Muscle soreness
2 Go really fast
3 Explosive material: Abbr.
4 Freudian concern
5 Swindler
6 Military doll
7 Like the Sahara desert
8 Actress Patti
15 "It Had To ___ You"

16 Shows that cost extra money
17 Opposite of down
18 Half-open
19 Blockhead
20 Da Vinci's "Mona ___"
21 Soak in the sun
24 Not old
25 Scheduled to arrive

PUZZLE 26

ACROSS

1 Young girl
5 Decline
8 Nitwit
10 "Golly!"
11 Actress Reed
12 Dog's snarl
13 ___ and tonic (drink)
14 Parting word
15 Advanced award in karate
18 Urban music with a heavy beat
19 Beverage containing caffeine
20 "Who am ___ disagree?"
21 Waiting in the wings
24 What we breathe
25 Get one's goat
26 Compass point: Abbr.
27 It's used to catch animals

DOWN

1 Cover for a jar
2 "Much ___ About Nothing"
3 Asian nation
4 Pertaining to sound
5 Kitchen utensil
6 Hard mineral
7 Flat, round cap
9 Casual shirt with wide shoulder straps
15 Football's Piccolo
16 Language spoken in ancient Rome
17 Poet Stephen Vincent ___
22 Gardner of the movies
23 Energy and vigor

ACROSS

1 Fellow student
10 Thirty-hour-a-week worker
11 "Carmen" watcher
12 Complain continually
13 Pain in the neck
16 "Uh uh"
17 Actress in "Butterfly"
23 College one graduates from
24 Pizza topping

DOWN

1 TV's "___ Sharkey"
2 Once around a track
3 ". . . why ___ you rich?"
4 It broke the camel's back
5 Alias used by an actor
6 Russian fighter plane
7 I love: Latin
8 Letter after ess
9 Blow it
14 "___" O'Reilly of "M*A*S*H"
15 Pic
17 Mush
18 ___-de-France
19 Music system component
20 Mute an ad with the remote
21 Stimpy's cartoon colleague
22 Greek shipper Onassis

PUZZLE 28

ACROSS

1 Small lie
4 Exclamation of disgust
9 Indignation
10 Hawaiian hello
11 Garfield's owner
12 Settle a loan
13 Private jest
15 Comedian Caesar
16 Kid's sleeping clothes
19 Solid carbon dioxide
22 Skater Henie
25 Cat hair
26 Kind of committee
27 Org. that Hoover ran
28 TV doctor Marcus
29 Tibetan ox

DOWN

1 Island country south of Samoa
2 Actor Jeremy
3 Dog movie of '74
4 Stop the car and remove the key
5 One of the Seven Dwarfs
6 Bounce like a bunny
7 "Gotcha!"
8 "___ cool!" (extremely hip)
14 Hat-throwing James Bond villain
17 In a ___ (taking little time)
18 Type of diving equipment
20 Somewhat sexy
21 Estrada of "CHiPs"
22 Wood-cutting tool
23 Lyric poem
24 Boston Bruins' org.

PUZZLE 29

ACROSS

1 Beer barrels
5 Folksinger Joan
9 Land-measure unit
10 Look leeringly at
11 Having zero money
13 Band leader Kyser
14 Drilling equipment
15 "I gave ___ the office"
16 "For ___ a Jolly Good Fellow"
17 State next to NH
19 Waterproof raincoat
20 Air blower
21 Engine part
24 Soft slime
25 Edge of a roof
26 Consider
27 Cain's brother

DOWN

1 Author Franz
2 Renown
3 Between black and white
4 "On your mark, get ___, go!"
5 Tennis star Becker
6 Excited
7 Large deer
8 Last letter
12 Hair-care name
16 Sheik's women
17 Delicate purple
18 California baseball player
19 Labyrinth
20 Love handles, e.g.
21 Layer of earth
22 Detective-story pioneer
23 "The Princess and the ___"

PUZZLE 30

ACROSS

1 Ceased dozing
6 Finished
8 Fascinated
9 Fisherman's bait
11 Policeman
12 "Voyage to the Bottom of the ___"
13 Negative prefix
14 Not out
15 Business neckwear
17 Compass direction: Abbr.
18 Old Testament book
20 Atkins of country music
21 Ruler of a vast domain
23 Becker, on "L.A. Law"

DOWN

1 At the peak
2 Move back and forth, as a tail
3 "Not ___ your life!"
4 Famed British gardens
5 Son of Seth
6 Feel anguish
7 Author of "Sister Carrie"
8 Very serious
10 French Impressionist painter
16 Housewife humorist Bombeck
17 Foot covering
19 Month after Mar.
20 ___ de coeur
22 Fourteenth letter

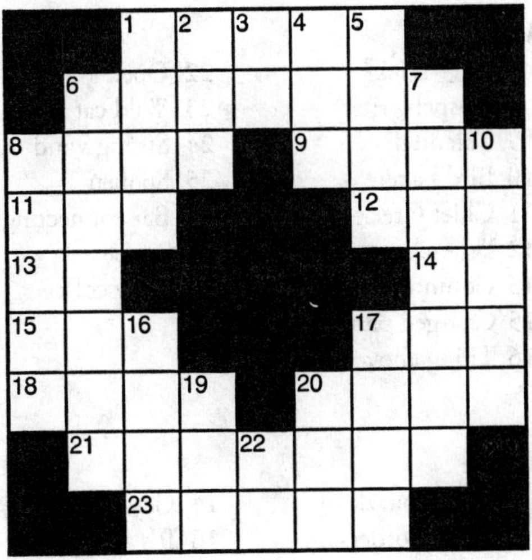

ACROSS

1 "___ Dick"
5 Gospel writer
9 Talented
10 Bird baker?
11 Chief Greek god
12 Where to get gold
13 Common cosmetic
15 Charged particle
16 Thing above attack

22 Open a little
23 Wild cat
24 Strong wind
25 Spoken
26 Bar connecting wheels
27 Brew coffee

DOWN

1 Pencil puzzle
2 Follow orders
3 Sky color
4 "Absolutely!"
5 The folks
6 Eager
7 Nevada city
8 Grasped mentally

14 Garden tool
16 It's a long story
17 Comet competitor
18 Use the phone
19 Restore to health
20 Actor Sharif
21 "___ on the Wild Side"

ACROSS

1 Environment: pref.
4 Layer of paint
8 Biblical boat
9 Light, hard wood
10 Big body of water
11 Assumed name
12 Excited shout
13 Happening
14 Real estate abbr.
15 Be in the red
16 TV program interrupter
17 Single magazine
19 Hockey great Bobby
20 Ups and ___
21 Hit the slopes
22 Official order
23 Hollywood's Ullmann
24 Great anger
25 Half of two

DOWN

1 Nicholson / Fonda film
2 Soft drink
3 Authorize
4 Have a cow
5 Andy Taylor's son
6 "Catch-22" actor
7 Try out a car
9 "I'm No Angel" star
15 One-sixteenth of a pound
18 Great gulp
19 Norway's capital

PUZZLE 33

ACROSS

1 Alphabet start
4 Neck warmer
9 Animal house?
10 Emulate a dragonfly
11 "Tea for ___"
12 Sinuous
13 "A mouse!"
14 Racer Unser
15 It's vanilla-flavored
20 Beside
21 Strike suddenly
22 An arm or a leg
25 Kind of code
26 Quiver item
28 Under the weather
29 Actress Davis
30 Watch carefully

DOWN

1 Cortez conqueree
2 Arbor
3 Journalist Alistair
4 "Pipe down!"
5 Hoods
6 Gardner of film
7 Race, as an engine
8 Boil in oil
14 Jimmy Carter's daughter
16 Monastery master
17 Harriet's husband
18 Like many a newspaper
19 Eve's offering
22 Kind of retriever, for short
23 Wrath
24 "A-Team" actor
27 "Shall ___ dance?"

ACROSS

1 Culkin film
10 Ancient kingdom
11 Orioles' home
12 Eisenhower, for short
13 "What about it?"
14 O'Hara's home
16 Adds up
20 So, la, ___ …
22 Grab forty winks
23 Italian tenor
27 Love goddess
28 "Absolutely!"

DOWN

1 Nun's garment
2 Japanese seaport
3 Long-distance runner
4 Consume
5 Author Kingsley
6 Long rides?
7 Yoko ___
8 Partner of "neither"
9 Before, to poets of yore
15 Video-game maker
17 Remove ropes from
18 Photo finish?
19 Caught sight of
21 Commonest metal
23 Wages
24 "The Naked ___"
25 Taping sys.
26 Peculiar

PUZZLE 35

ACROSS

1 Cancel
8 Flying, as a field
10 Southwestern cooking style
11 Actor Asner
13 Precious jewel
14 Agent's org.
15 France, way back when
17 Penicillin source
18 Kind of vase
19 Kind of sail
20 Pa's partner
21 Bogie costar
24 "___ Down Broadway"
26 Place to clean clothes

DOWN

1 Be a stool pigeon
2 Arden of film
3 Revolver type
4 Desert "ship"
5 Entry on a list
6 Put the kibosh on
7 "___ the Right Thing"
9 Simon or Sedaka
12 Pop
14 Shade of blue
15 Something to chew on
16 Bedouin, e.g.
17 Bible book
19 Sports cars, for short
21 It can have a crush on you
22 Role played by 11-Across
23 Tennis stroke
25 Pained cry

PUZZLE 36

ACROSS

1 What things cost
7 Buffalo-Albany connector
10 Michigan native
11 Potato bud
12 Boundary of bushes
13 Violinist's need
14 Copy closely
17 George Gershwin's brother
20 Neither win nor lose
22 Airplane reservation choice
23 Assent

DOWN

1 Heap
2 Gun, as an engine
3 Rink game
4 Rod of baseball
5 Author Bagnold
6 Vocalized
7 Ram's fan?
8 Acuff of country music
9 Director Spike
13 Onion-topped roll
14 OMB employee
15 Showy flower
16 Small, high plateau
17 Currier's colleague
18 Actor Stephen
19 Hill dweller
21 Compass pt.

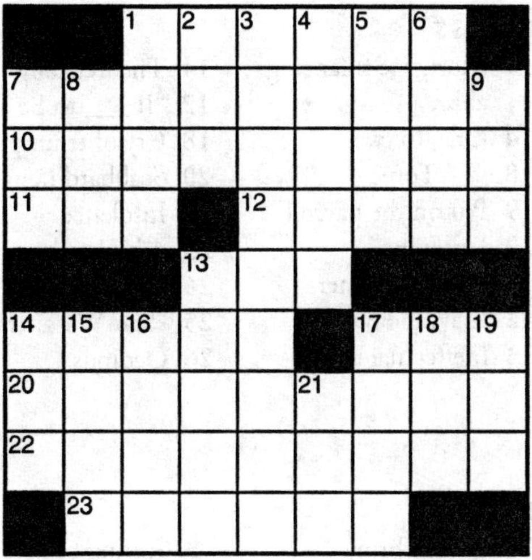
1 2 3 4 5 6
7 8 9
10
11 12
13
14 15 16 17 18 19
20 21
22
23

ACROSS

1 Mortgage financing abbr.
4 One, to two
8 ___ Tome
9 Put on the payroll
10 Lessening
11 Furry swimmer
12 Clay, today
13 Ineffectual thing
14 Theoretically
17 "It ___ to Be You"
18 Cry of triumph
20 Scabbard item
22 Insolence
23 A bit bonkers
24 WSW opp.
25 "Star Wars" character
26 Oedipus ___

DOWN

1 On the briny
2 Picasso or Casals
3 Errol Flynn role
4 Ask for money
5 Painting purveyor
6 Martial-arts master
7 New Deal pres.
9 Surfing bum
15 Hooded jacket
16 Liechtenstein border
19 Peak
20 Wild blue yonder
21 Seek as a spouse

ACROSS

1 Judge's specialty
4 Run off at the mouth
7 Brotherly baseball name
9 Wander about
10 Horse home
11 Slack-jawed
12 Jot
14 What a cow chews
15 Free, as services
19 Othello, for one
20 Clamorous
22 Second word of a story
23 Goof off
24 Lapidary's love
25 Question start

DOWN

1 Edison's workplace
2 "Oh, woe!"
3 Early bird's catch?
4 Boo-Boo's buddy
5 Cosmetics company
6 Place to hang one's hat
8 Mythical animal
9 4 Seasons hit
13 Make a knight
15 Bishop of Rome
16 "A ___ With a View"
17 Webster of words
18 Greek liqueur
19 Coffee cup
21 Morning moisture

ACROSS

1 First gardener?
5 Lacking stiffness
9 City famous for beans
10 It's often served with wine
11 "All About ___"
12 Unreturnable serve
13 Kitchen device
17 Masseur's need
18 Swing classic
24 Drag behind
25 Elegant resort
26 Guitarist Clapton
28 Prepare for a project
29 "___ happy returns!"
30 Food fish

DOWN

1 Actor Guinness
2 Prima donna
3 "You said it!"
4 NY neighbor
5 Sixteen oz.
6 Tehran's country
7 "Eek!" provokers
8 Kind of group
14 Exclamation of delight
15 Easy as ___
16 Hard wood
18 Romantic couple
19 "Doll" in " A Doll's House"
20 "___ Peaks"
21 Scandinavian capital
22 October birthstone
23 Hamlet, for one
27 Pitching great Young
28 "___ I Love You"

1 2 3 4 5 6 7 8
9 10
11 12
13 14 15 16
17
18 19 20 21 22 23
24 25
26 27 28
29 30

ACROSS

1 Bewildered by a blow
6 Schuss or telemark
9 Cooking by-product
10 Roofing material
11 Fall flat
12 Sham
13 Light axe
15 Tic-___-toe
16 Supersentimentalism
21 Grant of the movies
22 Stolen item
23 Tabloid topic
24 Dominican, for one
25 Service site
26 Part of MGM

DOWN

1 A bit bonkers
2 Folksinger Guthrie
3 Go like the wind
4 Fellow feeling
5 Nyet opposite
6 Pack away
7 Put foot to football
8 Pen filler
12 Grim or gruesome
14 Noah's second son
16 Not out
17 Blow one's own horn
18 Cafe au ___
19 Russian ruler of old
20 Actor Mostel
21 Eight ounces
24 Kind of radio sta.

ACROSS

1 Cutting comment
5 Malone of "Cheers"
8 Felipe, Jesus, or Matty
9 Single thickness
10 Rock ridge
11 Give up
12 Washington, ___
13 "Born on the ___ of July"
15 Pilot's place
16 Wordy
18 Boxing bout abbr.
20 Bonkers
21 Leave out
23 Acorn, in time
24 Salad ingredient
25 Be a busybody
26 "East of ___"

DOWN

1 Epic poet
2 Actor Baldwin
3 Wade's opponent
4 Lake Erie city
5 Scorn
6 Touched down
7 Story of the gods
11 Cervantes' "Don ___"
14 ___-Wan Kenobi
15 Jauntily conceited
16 Drop heavily
17 Crowd noise
18 Tarzan's transport
19 Mikita of Hockey
22 "Your name will be ___!"

ACROSS

1 Bird call
6 Rock requirement
9 Telecast's sound portion
10 Brock of baseball
11 Fork part
12 Mont Blanc, for one
13 Kipling's "Just ___ Stories"
14 Cartographic concern
15 1970 tear-jerker
19 Alien vehicle, for short
20 A note to follow "la"
21 Ruminant's mouthful?
22 Account entries
26 Put a question to
27 Kiss target
28 "The Old Man and the ___"
29 Shade of green

DOWN

1 Casual headgear
2 Epic movie "Ben-___"
3 Spinster's last words?
4 Get the dirt out
5 Bounder's toy
6 San Antonio site
7 Grinding tooth
8 Litter member
15 "Star Wars" director
16 Helpful
17 Colorless liquor
18 Tenth part
23 Slippery creature
24 Singer Torme
25 "Cabin in the ___"

ACROSS

1 Bluish-green
5 Baby bedwear
8 Windowpane holder
10 Funnyman Costello
11 Jeweled headdress
12 Royal flush card
13 "Lola" rock group
15 Grab some rays
16 Glib and deceptive speech

21 Well fluid
22 Pen pals?
24 Go on a run
25 Buzzing musical instrument
26 Rye topping
27 Betray boredom

DOWN

1 Likely
2 Hang it up
3 Jazz's state
4 Not moving
5 Architect's drawing
6 Gym rat
7 Brings action against
9 Fur trade center

14 Kind of
16 Relax with a rod
17 "My Way" lyricist
18 Glance through
19 Ms. Minnelli
20 Grasp mentally
23 Very long time

PUZZLE 44

ACROSS

1 Scamp
7 Song of the South
8 Wet blanket
11 Fuse blower
12 Business abbr.
13 Wilson's predecessor
14 Seafood platter item
16 "What's ___, Doc?"
17 Weight lifter
18 Common sailor
21 Large, covered porch
22 Imaginary

DOWN

1 Give new form to
2 Unwilling to mingle
3 Brief burst
4 Uncovered wagon
5 Venomous viper
6 Mary's TV boss at WJM
9 Community shocker
10 Two or three
11 Poker variation
14 Fad
15 Tenor Mario
17 Burn a bit
19 Brains of a computer: Abbr.
20 Relatives

ACROSS

1 Tell white lies
4 Nightclothes, familiarly
7 "David Copperfield" name
11 Chubby character actor
12 Sneaky
13 "___ the season . . ."
14 Mimic
15 Of the Middle Ages
21 Willis/Basinger film
22 Electric guitarist's need
23 Painter Avery

DOWN

1 "Are we having ___ yet?"
2 Anger
3 Compete in an auction
4 House animal
5 Shade of black
6 Catch sight of
8 Voluntarily do without
9 Landing site
10 Hick from the sticks
15 HBS degree
16 Shade tree
17 Buffet offering
18 Large container
19 ". . . I ___ the whole thing!"
20 ___ Luthor (Superman foe)

PUZZLE 46

ACROSS

1 Air rifle pellet
3 Very loud, in music: abbr.
5 Alley ___
7 Eastern religious path
8 Ring match
10 Leap
11 Type of torch
13 Composure
14 Left
16 Make messy
17 ___ and void
19 It has hops
20 Author Buscaglia
21 Very soft, in music: abbr.
22 Twenty, to Caesar

DOWN

1 Quick curtsy
2 Animated Betty
3 Musical movie of 1980
4 Fancy dresser
6 Goal
7 Melodious
9 Roger and Jessica Rabbit, e.g.
10 "Friday the 13th" antihero
12 Blackbird location?
14 Swallow hastily
15 Make a muscle
16 Chart territory
18 Bagel topping

ACROSS

1 Housewife or house-husband
10 Total agreement
11 Drought-ender?
12 Non-exploding bomb
13 Sort
15 "___ For Evidence"
17 Where sleepers go
23 Fuel transporter
24 Greatness

DOWN

1 Ben-___
2 "___ Clear Day . . ."
3 Hired help
4 Weariness with life
5 Go-between
6 "I ___ Camera"
7 Kith and ___
8 List-ending abbreviation
9 Livestock feed
14 Pottery ovens
16 Short-story writer
17 Hammerstein's "Why ___ Love You?"
18 Basketball hoop
19 Popular street name
20 Chewed and swallowed
21 After expenses
22 Finish the dishes

ACROSS

1 Pillow place
4 Kinda kooky
9 Have a marker out
10 Ben, on "Bonanza"
11 Ms. Fitzgerald
13 Barbie's beau
14 ___ Alamos
15 Rank below capt.
16 Fun-in-the-sun toy
20 "Er . . ."
21 Baby bear
22 Bit of a bite
24 Take by force
27 Go up
29 Madhouse
30 Therefore
31 English-language omega

DOWN

1 Dickens pseudonym
2 Lamb's kin
3 Singer-actress Reese
4 Photo illuminator
5 Biblical interjection
6 Flood craft
7 Ring slowly and solemnly
8 Streisand movie
12 Disney dwarf
16 "The Brady ___"
17 Rousseau character
18 School transport
19 Full of activity
23 Hazard in a new shirt
25 Richard of court fame
26 Big name in horror writing
28 Act introducer: abbr.

ACROSS

1 Assert
6 VH1's parent co.
9 Motorcycle maker
10 Sweater girl?
11 Pretentiously picturesque
12 Famous fort
13 Divided country
15 Myself and I companion
16 Speak with forked tongue
17 Re follower
19 Hose holder
21 The "Iliad," for one
23 Give a name to
24 Storage receptacle
25 Sugar source
26 Garden spot
27 Unexpected defeat

DOWN

1 Author Potok
2 Star of "M"
3 Put a penny in the pot
4 Pleasing and simple
5 Mom alternative
6 Repair
7 Only even prime number
8 Irritate
12 Patella
14 Basketball center?
17 Director Louis
18 Small bay
19 Come upon
20 Atlas contents
21 Get weaker
22 Crusted dessert
25 Greek letter

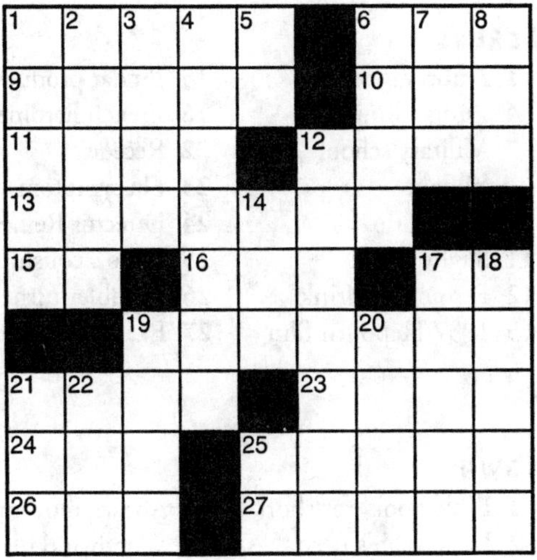
1
2
3
4
5
6
7
8
9
10
11
12
13
14
15
16
17
18
19
20
21
22
23
24
25
26
27

ACROSS

1 Actor Vigoda
4 Budget limit
7 Military school student
10 Indignatio
11 Slight trace
12 Fermented drink
13 1937 Hepburn film
15 Pindar product
16 French heroine
22 Recede
23 Flu symptom
24 Director Reiner
25 Bilbo's cousin
26 Tumbler turner
27 Excited exclamation

DOWN

1 Bible book, for short
2 Fisherman's need
3 Millay of poetry
4 "Catch you later!"
5 Woody's son
6 Equal
8 Urge
9 Really mad
14 Postpone
16 Abrupt movement
17 Woodwind instrument
18 Dear ___ (advice column)
19 State strongly
20 Make over
21 Raven or rook

1	2	3				4	5	6
7			8	9		10		
11						12		
13					14			
			15					
16	17	18				19	20	21
22				23				
24				25				
26						27		

ACROSS

1 Florida city
6 Confer a rank upon
9 Be ready for
10 Letter after pi
11 International alliance
12 America, for short
13 He played Gomer Pyle
17 "Ishtar" director
20 Large-beaked bird
21 Gung-___
22 Servants
26 Beast of burden
28 Chef Child
29 Court divider
30 Packing a gun

DOWN

1 Bar bill
2 Hole-making tool
3 Chinese chairman
4 Outdoors meal
5 "Breakfast ___ Tiffany's"
6 Med. title
7 Kirk's colleague
8 Cow nickname
14 Santa ___
15 1959 Heston film
16 Chanted word
17 "___ Frome"
18 Unconfined
19 "___ contraire!"
23 Common lawn tree, once
24 Prevaricate
25 Hippie's home
27 Ave. crosser
28 Yes, in Hamburg

ACROSS

1 Act angry
5 Cotton quantity
9 Dry and barren
10 Put up a stink?
11 ___-tac-toe
12 Eager or excited
13 Corn serving
14 Woolly mama
15 Bar item
19 Funny fellow
20 Zilch
21 Greek hero
23 R followers
24 Cooing creature
25 "___ of Flying"
26 Action
27 Lawman Wyatt

DOWN

1 Goddesses who control destiny
2 Mr. Wickfield's clerk Heep
3 Speedy oven
4 Phys ___ (gym class)
5 Noisy quarrel
6 Arm of the Mediterranean
7 Writer Tolstoy
8 Ticker tape?: abbr.
14 Omelet requirement
16 Put a strain on
17 Indian instrument
18 Drink noisily
21 Make two and two equal four
22 Namath or Montana
25 Santa ___

PUZZLE 53

ACROSS

1 Three-point kick
10 Reasoned conclusion
11 Maryland city
12 Cleopatra's killer
13 Freud interest
14 Funny fellow
16 They've replaced LPs
17 "To be ___ not to be?"
18 Comedian Kabibble
20 Place to find fodder
25 Himalayan mountain range
26 Child's stuffed toy

DOWN

1 Lie a little
2 "Time ___ Bottle"
3 Black key
4 Allows
5 Trickle down
6 Ruby or diamond
7 Lennon's wife
8 Sharp-smelling
9 Yorkshire city
14 "Hawaii Five-O" villain
15 "Goodnight, ___"
16 Tedious task
18 Early Cosby show
19 Returned part of a ticket
21 Bring to a finish
22 Mom's mate
23 Cell component: Abbr.
24 In one ___ and out the other

ACROSS

1 Wheat husks
6 Agent's org.
9 Unconfirmed report
10 Bolt
11 Worship
12 Feedback source
13 Offspring
14 Lead symbol
15 Monopoly square
16 PC competitor
18 ___ art

20 It's E of MT
22 "Dead Souls" writer
24 Noh wear
25 She could have danced all night
26 Stream stopper
27 With stateliness
28 Batik essential
29 Tamarind and tangerine

DOWN

1 Food expert Claiborne
2 Arm of the Atlantic
3 "Roots" actor John
4 Discussion location
5 One not tied to a team
6 Hubbub

7 Dupe
8 Diminutive demon
17 Turn red
19 Dramas
21 Stop on a ___
23 Cutting comment
24 Out of the ordinary

ACROSS

1 Toy manufacturer?
4 Gush forth
8 "Billy, Don't ___ Hero"
9 Take a long look
10 Wagered
11 Sports championship
12 Made with artistry
14 Rugged and uneven

15 Started a Model T
17 "Home on the ___"
18 The fifty states: abbr.
21 Curved up, then down
22 Tease a little
23 Keg contents
24 Football position

DOWN

1 "___ Tide" (Righteous Brothers hit)
2 Marvin of movies
3 "Ha!"
4 Suppress
5 "The Miracle Worker" actress

6 Perry's creator
7 Pesky plant
9 Pursued prey
13 Fraudulent substitute
15 Zodiac creature
16 Extremely unusual
19 Offense against God
20 Append

ACROSS

1 Gift-wrapping garnish
4 Lummox
5 In medias ___
6 Capital
12 "Husbands and Wives" actress
13 Fit to eat
14 VIII x XIII
15 Poetic night
16 Lion lair

DOWN

1 Shameless
2 Spy
3 "A Nightmare on Elm Street" director
6 He decides what's fair
7 Zadora of film
8 Chum
9 Ivan Boesky, for one
10 Costa Del ___
11 Maa ma'am

ACROSS

1 North American Indian
7 ___ Louis Cardinals
9 The "Queen of Soul"
10 Cry of surprise
11 Church instrument
13 Depart
14 Kind of hunt
18 California county
19 Grass substitute
24 In the matter of
25 Perfect place
26 Hall-of-Famer Cobb
27 Device to detect phenomena

DOWN

1 Atlas item
2 "Either he goes ___ go!"
3 With-it
4 Put away
5 It lasts four beats
6 Singer Carpenter
7 Use a razor
8 Copier need
12 Monkeyshine
14 Brainy
15 Baseball's Stengel
16 Show pieces
17 Computer problem
20 Two thousand pounds
21 Raises
22 Seaport, for short
23 Nowhere near

PUZZLE 58

ACROSS

1 Owns
4 Serious play
9 Farm worker?
10 Dog name
11 Last letter
12 Bring down
13 Female sheep
14 Leave
15 "Ridiculous!"
16 Picture
19 "A Star ___ Born"
21 Common article
22 Bullring cry
25 Tolkien creature
27 Blend together
28 Jacket part
29 Pod contents
30 Foe
31 Use a kazoo

DOWN

1 Harass a pledge
2 Once more
3 Rising sharply
4 Hovering insect
5 Man-like machine
6 Actress Gardner
7 Merge smoothly
8 Region
17 Sheik's concubines
18 Vim
19 Not working
20 White waterfowl
23 In ___ of (for)
24 Checkup
26 Gibbon, e.g.

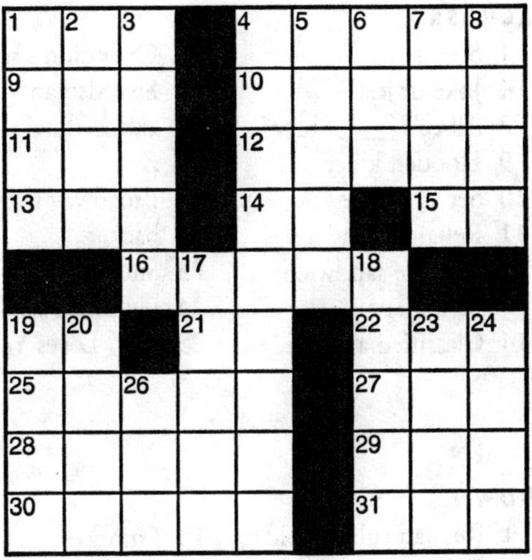
1 2 3 4 5 6 7 8
9 10
11 12
13 14 15
16 17 18
19 20 21 22 23 24
25 26 27
28 29
30 31

PUZZLE 59

ACROSS

1 Shout
4 Joke or jest
8 Albee's "___ Story"
9 Hooded killer
10 Set as a price
11 Religious leader
12 Possible sandwich ingredient
14 Classified ad abbr.
15 Operation's start time
20 Swordsman extraordinaire
21 X
22 Broadway show backer
23 Short flight
24 Unskilled worker
25 "___ Loves You"

DOWN

1 Russian ruler of old
2 Optimistic
3 Symbol of servitude
4 Actress Williams
5 Israel's Eban
6 Poke
7 Ingest
9 Gas-saving group
13 Empty
15 "The Twilight ___"
16 Therefore
17 Folk singer Phil
18 "Oops!"
19 Ready to pick
20 Comic-strip sound

PUZZLE 60

ACROSS
1 Novelist Levin
4 Conducting rod
9 "Othello" heroine
11 Wimbledon winner
12 Small lump
13 "Drive, ___ Said"
14 Avignon article
15 R & B artist Redding
18 Do needlework?
21 Yours truly
22 In ___
23 Hemingway's nickname
25 First name in fashion
27 "The Sound of Music" song
29 Aplomb
30 Corroded

DOWN
1 Gem state
2 Bowling alley button
3 Bat material
4 Exist
5 Take a stroll
6 "Ready for renting"
7 Lennon's assumed middle name
8 Collar
10 ___ minimus
16 Kennedy Airport architect
17 Barkers?
19 Summit
20 Author of "Steppenwolf"
23 Vim and vigor
24 "Oklahoma!"'s Annie
25 "O Come, All ___ Faithful"
26 By means of
28 Us guys

ACROSS

1 Bouillabaisse base
6 Locomotive
10 Twain character
11 Full of sugar
12 Anvil location
13 Disapproving
   expression
15 Manipulate
18 Squabbles
22 Lacking light
24 Really hurting
25 Pitiless

DOWN

1 Projecting edge
2 Eternal City
3 Commencement
4 "Everything is settled
   now!"
5 Question word
6 "___ a Wonderful
   Life"
7 Kind of bread or
   whiskey
8 At ___ (bewildered)
9 Make a mistake
14 Familiar form of
   address
15 News service: Abbr.
16 Soul stain
17 Zeta follower
19 Baby buck
20 Noisy fight
21 Pie in the ___
23 "Murder, She Wrote"
   network

PUZZLE 62

ACROSS

1 Where rays meet
5 Bang, as a toe
9 Daily need
10 Migratory worker
11 Refresh one's memory
13 Horse's feeder
14 Slumberwear, familiarly
16 From ___ Z
17 Rollicking square dance
21 Last call
24 Meter's eater
25 Anatomical hinge
26 Bronte heroine
27 Roof edge

DOWN

1 Stretch the truth
2 Bobby of hockey
3 One who gives advice
4 Not ___ many words
5 "Melrose Place" actor
6 Head honcho
7 German sinker
8 What a beatnik beats, perhaps
12 Usual U. prereq.
14 Something kids go through
15 "For he's a ___ good fellow"
18 See regularly
19 ___-Gyn
20 Stopped sleeping
22 Clergyman: Abbr.
23 Brown of the Celtics

PUZZLE 63

ACROSS

1 "There oughta be a ___!"
4 "60 Minutes" network
7 Brightly-colored perennial
9 Home, to Aeneas
10 Home, to the Minotaur
11 Song some sing Sunday
12 Kind of kid's gun
13 The fear of God

15 Opposite of AD
16 Roll of cash
17 Actress Derek
19 Detective-agency symbol
20 "One if ___ land, . . ."
22 Competent
24 Fictional Jane
26 Badger's buddy
27 Milking need
28 Put a spell on
29 Moxie

DOWN

1 Out on a ___
2 "West Side Story" role
3 Expert
4 Show sorrow
5 Failed show
6 In ___ (meshing well)
8 Beach sight
9 Book by Benchley

14 Method
17 Where you'll be in hot water
18 Hautboy, today
20 Appetizer cheese
21 Short, sharp shout
23 Over easy
25 Short, sharp bark

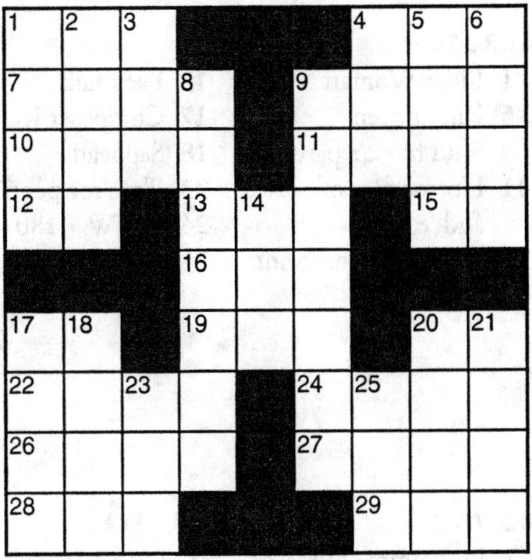
1
2
3
4
5
6
7
8
9
10
11
12
13
14
15
16
17
18
19
20
21
22
23
24
25
26
27
28
29

ACROSS

1 Little Woman
5 Fairy queen
8 Stud horse's partner
11 Horror film of '42 and '82
12 Personal manservant
13 Back talk
17 Composer Kurt
18 Saphead
23 Place for pennies
24 WNW + 180 degrees
25 Circular current

DOWN

1 Programme purveyor: Abbr.
2 Period of note
3 Small child
4 Baseball bounce
5 Joplin's "___ Leaf Rag"
6 Van Gogh worked there
7 Borscht base
9 Evildoing
10 Sound of sorrow
13 Rip off
14 Sponsorship
15 Burn a bit
16 Wearily wend one's way
19 "Honest ___"
20 Crazy
21 Sturm ___ Drang
22 Aurora area

PUZZLE 65

ACROSS

1 Do the grass
4 Each
7 Baltimore's state: Abbr.
9 It's used for navigation
11 Ways out
12 One-time Beatle Sutcliffe
13 Expression of dismay
14 Fancy
15 Box-score heading
16 Rainbow producer
17 Seattle Slew, e.g.
19 "That feels good!"
20 Laugh a little
21 Malted drink

DOWN

1 Subway
2 "There But For Fortune" songwriter
3 NBA Hall-of-Famer Unseld
4 Country between Spain and France
5 "The Mikado" character
6 Opposite to what might be expected
7 French painter Henri
8 Ringo Starr, for one
10 Casual coverup
14 Authored
16 Talk-show host Donohue
18 Greek letter

ACROSS

1 Find a total
4 Large amount of money
7 Speak lovingly
8 Uncouth person
9 Goal
10 Beta alternative
11 Tending
12 Nuclear physicist Enrico
14 Extra space
16 Transition
17 Go down a bit
18 Young man
19 Finish first
20 Box top
21 Took a loss
22 "... have you ___ wool?"
23 Nod meaning

DOWN

1 Without instrumental backing
2 Steely Dan hit
3 Comedian DeLuise
4 Go back and forth
5 Foam-born goddess
6 City on the Raccoon River
11 Boob
12 Doctor's charge
13 Devil's offspring
15 Reddish
19 Manner or style

ACROSS

1 Triangular sail
4 Crow cry
7 Pizza spice
9 Work hard at pleasing
10 Sounded ominously
11 Simile center
12 Dignified
16 Neighbor of Cameroon
17 Flying high
18 Hogan of golf
19 Sault ___ Marie

DOWN

1 Letterman
2 Persia, today
3 ___ noire
4 Noted astronomer
5 Aardvark, at times
6 Actress Natalie
8 Medicine capsule ingredient
12 One who puts on airs
13 Love god
14 Light, swingy rhythm
15 George Bush's alma mater

ACROSS

1 Tag on
4 "Right on the nose!"
9 Con's foe
10 Workers' collective
11 Trim twigs from a tree
12 Axe
13 Be obliged
14 Special skill
17 Steinem's magazine
18 One of the Hardy Boys
19 "...and a merry old soul was ___"
20 League rule
22 "Born Free" author Adamson
23 Imitator
24 Egyptian headdress creature
25 Wharton's Frome
27 Princess perturber
28 Becomes
29 His career is on the line

DOWN

1 Poise
2 Half asleep
3 Dummy
4 C&W artist
5 Pointless
6 Blues singer Simone
7 With 8-Down, continue
8 See 7-Down
15 Picked
16 Calculator part
18 What Perry opened
21 "Oz" actor
22 Taunt
25 With 26-Down, famous accusation
26 See 25-Down

PUZZLE 69

ACROSS

1 '75 Spielberg shocker
5 JFK's successor
8 Melancholy-toned instrument
9 Annuity alternative: Abbr.
10 Comedian Milton
12 Dance style
13 "___, lies, and videotape"
14 "Till ___ meet again"
15 Bridegroom's buddy
18 Efrem Zimbalist, ___
19 Not safe
20 Numskull
22 Peruvian pack animal
25 Kind of pole
26 Key point
27 Bring bad luck
28 Keep out of sight

DOWN

1 Famed sufferer
2 Justice Fortas
3 Inferior
4 Tennis star Monica
5 Burning
6 Muscular strength
7 Trick
11 Praise highly
15 Car stopper
16 Ground cover
17 Sega competitor
18 Kid
21 Put right
23 Wet earth
24 Cancel suddenly

ACROSS

1 COBOL relative
5 Fizz preceder?
9 "___ la Douce"
10 Hollywood's Turner
11 Circus employee
13 Set as a price
14 NM neighbor
15 Solo's shipmate
20 Baby doctor: Abbr.
21 Finsteraarhorn, for one
22 Awkward dive
26 Since
27 Like many tracks
28 Mendelian subject
29 Lap dog

DOWN

1 Pale purple
2 ___ setter
3 It comes out of chimneys
4 Kitchen container
5 Shopping center
6 Run for it
7 Loneliest number?
8 Between birdie and bogey
12 Striped cat
16 Fictional detective Nero
17 Birth a baby bovine
18 Dagger companion?
19 Pie ingredient
22 Piece of luggage
23 Compass dir.
24 Cambodian leader Nol
25 Coxcomb

ACROSS

1 Drinking gourd
10 Handy
11 With abundance
12 Lode load
13 "Kramer ___
   Kramer"
14 PO state
15 Payment for services
16 PO state
18 PO state
19 Progress record
20 King of Babylon
24 Barge way
25 Not customized

DOWN

1 "Hamlet"'s author?
2 Creamy white
3 Stare slack-jawed
4 CCLI + CCLI
5 Ball show
6 Short break
7 Home of "All Things
   Considered": abbr.
8 Wing
9 Curious George's
   creator
15 Well-known
16 Decay
17 Sprightly
19 Actress Turner
20 "And I Love ___"
21 Is plural?
22 Farrow of film
23 Hit head on

1	2	3	4	5	6	7	8	9
10								
11								
12			■	13		■		
14		■	15			■	16	17
■			18		■	19		
20	21	22			23			
24								
25								

ACROSS

1 Dress
5 Chick chirp
9 Tract
10 Tentmaker's son
11 Vim
12 Telegraph
13 Put away
14 Sandwich spread
15 Knowing
17 Wing it
19 Microwave
22 Title word
23 It often has one line
24 Office shape
25 Tennist Nastase
26 Beaver's pop
27 Steep slope

DOWN

1 Long look
2 "Celeste Aida," for one
3 Airport pickup
4 Porter's piece
5 Sway
6 Dreyfus supporter
7 Viscount's superior
8 The hunted
14 Pug's punch
16 Use as a weapon
17 State strongly
18 1982 French film
20 Similar
21 Cheat like a child
23 Boom of a derrick

ACROSS

1 Windy storm
8 Fonda film
10 Greeting
11 Noah's vessel
12 Southern state: abbr.
13 Pub drink
15 Actress Arthur
16 "Treasure Island" initials
17 Foreign car, for short
18 Mouth piece
19 Tony resort
20 For example: abbr.
21 Cereal sound?
24 Alternatively
25 Stock transaction
28 Cheat on

DOWN

1 Car indicator
2 Spielberg critter
3 Financial deg.
4 Average
5 Benevolent beast?
6 MO city
7 Indian carving
8 Basketball's Barkley
9 Not knowing
14 Tabloid topic
15 Certain shot
21 Favoring
22 Mel of Cooperstown
23 Greek letter
26 "That hurts!"
27 In the morning: abbr.

PUZZLE 74

ACROSS

1 Felidae family member
4 ___ du Diable
5 Solder ingredient
6 Tension-provoking
12 Rich dessert
13 "Unquestionably!"
14 Hodges or Santos
15 "How Can ___ Sure?"
16 "Miss Pym Disposes" author

DOWN

1 Lime genus
2 Weaver film
3 2, in 325
6 Humor magazine
7 Turning point in a ballet?
8 Professional penman
9 Actor Granger
10 Hula helper, for short
11 Spider-Man creator

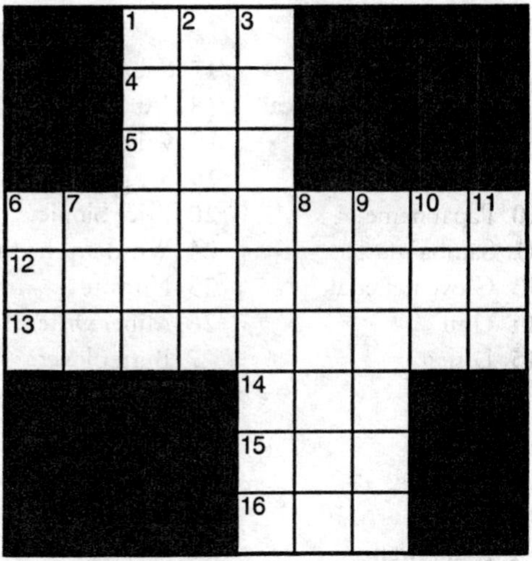

ACROSS

1 Rookie reporter
4 Type of hypothetical particle
9 Wrong, notewise
10 Papal name
11 Samba music
13 Glove material
14 Gun
15 Lose it
17 Subtle
18 "At Seventeen" songwriter
19 Sty guy
20 Brice biopic
24 Word on the first flag
25 No vote
26 Miner writer Brett
27 Butter lover?

DOWN

1 Male swan
2 Marsh gas?
3 Big name in Behaviorism
4 Campus locale
5 Keats subject
6 Australian Dream-Time believer, for one
7 Poe subject
8 Ten beater
12 Sample soda
15 Scotch amount
16 Mercer lyric
17 Confused state
19 Evil alter ego
21 Crooner Cole
22 Unedited
23 Sodium hydroxide

ACROSS

1 Want badly
8 With a leg on either side
9 Put into words
10 Intl. conglomerate
12 Sand land
13 Vulpine?
14 Debussy influence
16 Tipsy
17 Lock
18 NC neighbor
19 Attend
20 One who wassails
21 Plastic ingredient

DOWN

1 Safety strap
2 Presage
3 Narrow waterway
4 Beaten path
5 Tall tale
6 Coleridge composition
7 As regards
10 Sparkle like snow
11 Unsightly sight
13 "Remington ___ "
15 Suit material?
19 Macavity, e.g.
20 Forester or Lewis

ACROSS

1 Strikebreaker
5 Altar answer
8 Dancing style
9 Famed diarist
10 Crowd?
11 Explosive initials
12 Obnoxious one
13 Psychic mediator?
14 Short course
16 ___ Tin Tin
17 Sing the praises of
18 Append
19 Swordplay staple
20 The wild West?
21 Eye piece
22 Isr. neighbor
23 Thomas Waller, familiarly

DOWN

1 Webb role
2 Salsa spice
3 Growing up
4 Reading room?
5 Burial
6 Squalid quality
7 Successful
14 Small drinks
15 Pushy and impatient personality

ACROSS

1 Peter Lorre role
10 Cake kind
11 Measure of star luminance
12 Brachiator
13 Humorist Billings
16 Country's McEntire
20 Concerning
21 Ground grain
22 Catherine ___ (Henry VIII's 6th)
23 Italian river
24 Analogous
25 Bit of a battle
26 Kitten's handle
27 Lift

DOWN

1 Make it up, musically
2 "Strangers ___ Train"
3 Fool's facial?
4 "Stormy Weather" singer
5 Block from behind
6 Unpleasant consequence, sometimes
7 Marker
8 5 1/2 yards
9 Wordsworth work
13 See 14-Down
14 Seaport of 13-Down
15 "Peanuts," for one
17 Horripilating
18 Resort location
19 In flight

ACROSS

1 List punctuator
6 It takes the bait?
9 Lake Tana's location
10 Give the once-over
11 Draw back
15 Frat-party wear
16 Line game
20 Nicholson movie
21 Actor Dennehy

DOWN

1 Nicholson movie
2 "What have we here?"
3 Do the floors
4 "Are you referring to Miss Piggy?"
5 Rap sheet entry
6 Parker who played Boone
7 Septennial sensation?
8 Light carriage
12 Emulated Arachne
13 "The African Queen" scriptwriter
14 Gridiron gain
16 Kid
17 Act human?
18 "___ Hear a Waltz?"
19 Geneticist's initials

ACROSS

1 Joke
5 Frolic
9 "Back to you"
10 Devilish doing
11 Lloyd's son
12 Tibetan monk
13 Bibliography phrase
15 Ancestor of 18-Across
17 Actress Wray
18 High-tech music medium
19 Gardner pseudonym
21 Calm in the storm
22 A ways away
26 Sorrowful sigh
27 Inflation accommodation: Abbr.
28 Finnegans' follower
29 Leave the stage

DOWN

1 Esther's successor
2 The night before
3 ___ of Tranquility
4 Test type
5 Baton competition
6 Ellipsoid
7 Act just like
8 Tartan-patterned
14 "___-Pan"
15 A. Becker's show
16 Singer Abdul
20 AA fire
23 New network
24 "Oklahoma!"'s Hakim
25 Hole maker

ACROSS

1 Casual greeting
6 Baby fox
9 More or less
10 Little Woman
11 Ira Levin play
13 Adolescent
14 Scrooge cry
16 Driver's need
17 Pacify
21 Jiffy
24 Ark passenger
25 Ezio role
26 Compass dir.
27 Radio and TV

DOWN

1 Suffered from
2 Author Kobo
3 Detestable
4 It's plucked
5 Will-wisp link
6 Macchio / Morita movie
7 Developer's concern
8 Melville novel
12 AK abutter
14 Wash down
15 Dam site
18 We, the people
19 Attention getter
20 Go or Go Fish
22 Gin man Whitney
23 Vast volume

PUZZLE 82

ACROSS

1 Impersonate
7 Elgar's "___ Variations"
8 Apollo or Ra
9 They work under-ground
11 Before marriage
12 "A zed & two noughts"
13 Ear piece
14 Scenery chewer
15 Gold-medalist Korbut
16 Stritch of Broadway
18 One buried in a book
19 Linen fabric

DOWN

1 Basil + garlic + oil
2 Difficult duty
3 Beelzebub's business
4 Yule drink
5 Slide sight
6 Nigerian pop singer
9 Flowering shrub
10 Polite refusal
13 Frequent filer
14 Roundup result
15 Small bills
17 G & S princess

ACROSS

1 Newborn need
5 Hines' hoofing hit
8 Slept like ___
9 "What did you say?"
10 Mixer
12 Cheryl, on "Charlie's Angels"
13 Firm but not soft
16 Moon sea
17 Egg-laying mammal
22 Standee's lack
23 Freedom from formality
24 She's often fleeced
25 High point

DOWN

1 Singer Davis
2 Indispose
3 Dan McGrew's love
4 CIS CIA
5 Sticker?
6 Go over the books
7 Aspect
11 Trapshooting target
13 Bounteous
14 Legal show
15 Cover with cloth
18 Verily
19 Oversimplified ideas
20 Take advantage of
21 Westheimer's field

ACROSS

1 "D.C. Cab" actor
4 Streaking, e.g.
7 Red letters?
8 Packed away
9 Boris's partner
11 Went off
12 School grp.

13 House soldiers
17 Address
18 Cal. page
19 Couple
20 Lodge member
21 Fitting

DOWN

1 Salt vault
2 Laugh loud and long
3 Degas drawing detail
4 It offers rapid advancement
5 Fundamentally
6 Lacking a dial tone

10 What one wears
13 Portend
14 Ethiopian princess of fiction
15 Sudden ouster
16 Speed unit

ACROSS

1 Decrease
7 "The Long Goodbye" director
8 Become revolting?
9 Quotidian
10 Belief
13 Dr. Zamenhof's invention
15 Winner in 1973
16 Tube type
17 Noble principles
18 Easily handled
19 Severe trial

DOWN

1 Makeup maker
2 Marty Robbins' #1 song
3 Rank indicator
4 1975 beauty-pageant film
5 Dennis Hopper directed it
6 Vane dir.
10 Natural-born
11 Stanley's cry
12 Bit of a bite
14 Put ___ to (stop)
17 "___ Crazy" (Paul Davis hit)

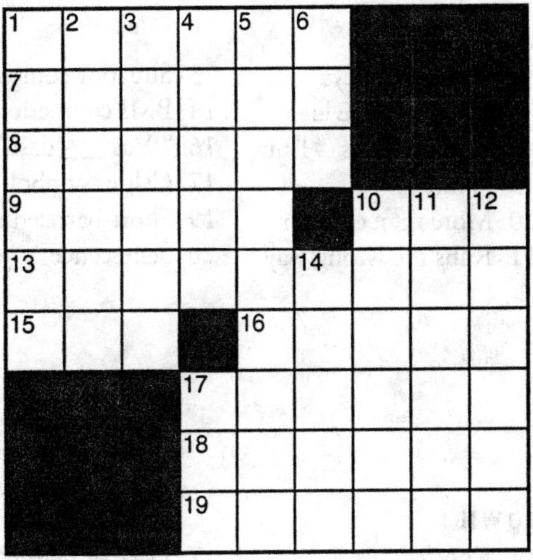
1 2 3 4 5 6
7
8
9 10 11 12
13 14
15 16
17
18
19

ACROSS

1 They have keys
7 Uncollectable loan
8 Hall & Oates' #1 hit
9 Whiff
10 More than enough
11 Rubs the wrong way

13 Superior companion?
14 BMI competitor
16 "Was ___ das?"
17 Celtics symbol
19 Short-barreled rifle
20 Senescence

DOWN

1 Knock
2 Piece of one's mind?
3 End of "South Pacific" song title
4 Cost after adjustments
5 Four-sided stone pillar
6 Mason's secretary

7 Piece of plastic?
8 Fire department head
9 Washout
12 Dance with a syncopated rhythm
15 Goody-two-shoes
18 Number of even primes

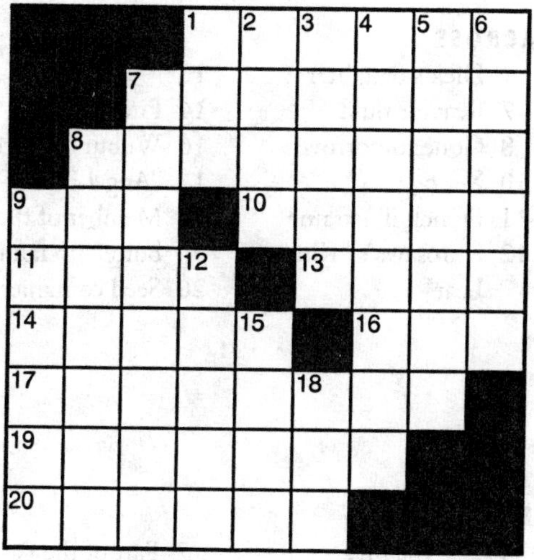

ACROSS

1 Dick's daughter
7 Reactor fluid
8 Gone tomorrow
10 Xeric
11 French illustrator
12 Kurosawa's "King Lear"
13 "___ note to . . ."
14 Pitched low
16 Wilbur and Freddy
17 "Angel Heart" actress
19 Member of the buttercup family
20 Seed container

DOWN

1 ___ the line
2 PC need
3 "___ Three Lives"
4 Monacan princess
5 Wrathful
6 In any event
7 Part of the Pacific
8 Cap piece
9 Nut-based candy
15 Pack firmly
16 Duck place
18 Crowd cry

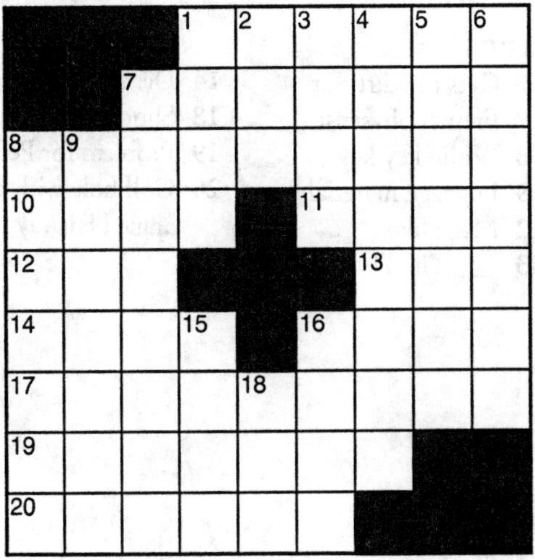
1
2
3
4
5
6
7
8
9
10
11
12
13
14
15
16
17
18
19
20

ACROSS

1 Gets the dirt out
7 French physicist
8 White key key
9 Luggage material
12 Make like
13 ___ Tin Tin
14 Deadpan
18 Short-tailed shorebird
19 Problem for Peru
20 Golf hole with an angled fairway

DOWN

1 Servicewomen: abbr.
2 Rambo's need
3 Nine inches
4 Flight
5 Creating concupiscence
6 Undisturbed
9 Weakened
10 Twin of Artemis
11 River of SE Asia
15 Theodicy concern
16 Director Clair
17 Hopper

ACROSS

1 "I placed ___ in Tennessee, . . ."
5 Sail support
9 Bound bundle
10 "Show Boat"'s Ferber
11 Revenged for a wrong
12 Place of refuge
13 Like some bond interest
15 Bad spells
16 Frank's ex
18 Swab down
21 Laze about
23 Of great extent
24 Defendant's response
25 Former NBAer Birdsong
26 Charon's river
27 Stimulate

DOWN

1 Help on a heist
2 Joe
3 "Roots" writer
4 Richards of court fame
5 Confused conflict
6 Economics giant
7 Cut quickly
8 Cutting
14 IV x V
16 Famous range
17 Fencing move
19 Jim Davis creation
20 Dennis, to Mr. Wilson
22 Careless
23 Impress mightily

PUZZLE 90

ACROSS

1 "___ Mice and Men"
3 Soldiers' org.
5 Else
6 Located at
7 Aussie actor
13 Come to an understanding
14 Make follow
15 Express
16 Violent outburst
18 Wire service?: Abbr.
19 Wynn or Norton
20 Greenlight
21 Lah-dah middle

DOWN

1 "Papa-___-mow-mow" (song of '62)
2 Abolitionist Douglass
3 Magenta or heliotrope
4 Andy's pal
8 Different drummer hearer
9 Social slip
10 Pedestal toppers
11 Beat topper
12 He was found guilty in 1921
16 ___ Schwarz
17 When the first vernacular hymnal appeared

ACROSS

1 Word taken from Arabic
10 Black and tan
11 Stamina exemplar
12 Pause filling
13 Harrison, in "Presumed Innocent"
14 Throwing ability
15 Bill of note
18 "Evening Shade" character
21 Gyroscopic instrument
23 Detailed
24 ". . . a jar in ___"

DOWN

1 Org. started in 1920
2 Lodge
3 "Here's ___!"
4 Gerund trailer
5 Bakery offering
6 Run-of-the-mill
7 "One of ___"
8 Unite
9 Adrenalized
14 Ornament
15 Sic dogs on
16 Futhark character
17 Env abbr.
18 "Eheu!"
19 Yes or no
20 To ___
22 Chip toppings: abbr.

1	2	3	4	5	6	7	8	9
10								
11								
12			■	13				
■	■	■	14			■	■	■
15	16	17			■	18	19	20
21				22				
23								
24								

ACROSS

1 Elastic
8 Vocal vibrato
9 Parks of '55
10 Cook Rombauer
13 Inclined
14 Great toughness
15 How follower
16 Show follower
17 Element after Cl
18 Walk with down the aisle
20 22.5 deg.
21 Ground item
22 Amonasro's daughter
23 Sided with?
25 Hide changer

DOWN

1 Layer
2 Plan
3 Symbol for silence
4 "___ ba-a-ad boy!"
5 Element after Md
6 Leonard book
7 Long ago
11 Phrygian flower
12 Even then
14 Lulu's love?
16 Ligurian lovely
19 Something to hold on to
20 Daughter of Styx
22 Actress Jillian
24 For each

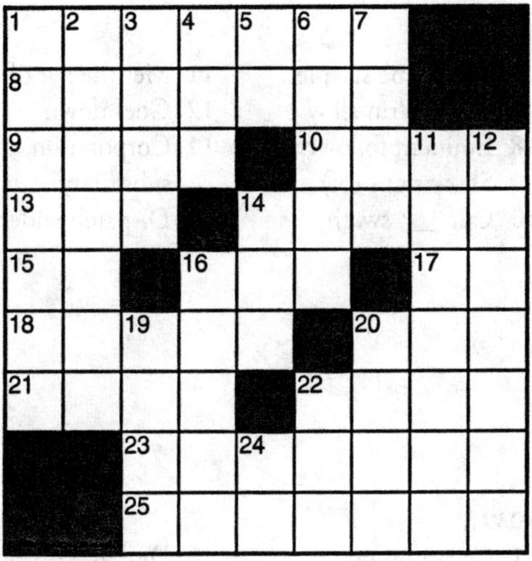
1
2
3
4
5
6
7
8
9
10
11
12
13
14
15
16
17
18
19
20
21
22
23
24
25

ACROSS

1 Like some steeples
7 Copper/tin alloy
8 Eminent follower
9 Show signs (of)
10 Cut ___ swath
11 Met the bet of
12 Goes down
14 Corporation, to a subsidiary
15 Dispatch ender

DOWN

1 Common mixer
2 Economical
3 Forwardness
4 Emulated a cataract
5 Nyro's comer
6 Dull grayish-brown
9 Type of journey
12 Quick
13 Cry of contempt

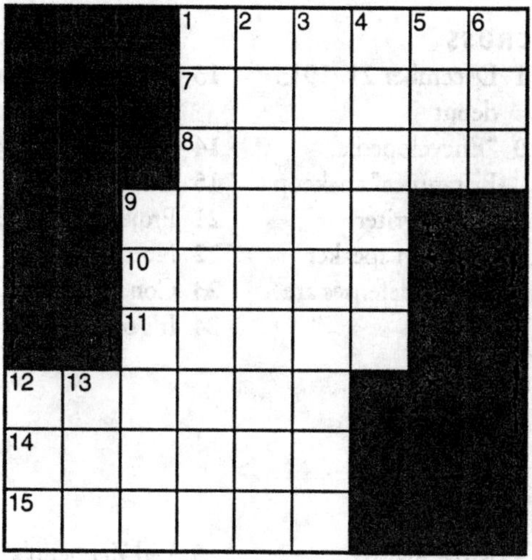
1
2
3
4
5
6
7
8
9
10
11
12
13
14
15

ACROSS

1 December 21, 1913 debut
10 "Encyclopedia Britannica" makeup article writer
11 Murngin speaker
12 Where defenses are set up
13 Wilson and Heath: Abbr.
14 Util.
15 Guarantee
21 Projecting range
22 Nun's life
23 Con
24 It's on the IJsselmeer

DOWN

1 Move swiftly
2 Chambers wear
3 ___ about
4 Authoritative and inviolable writing
5 Shine unsteadily
6 TGIF sayer
7 "Step ___!"
8 Clayton in "Benson"
9 Led Zeppelin's "___ Mak'er"
15 "Fraxinus" member
16 Bond, for example
17 Inf. opp.
18 Original Luddite
19 Org. established in 1947
20 Dicotyledonous tree

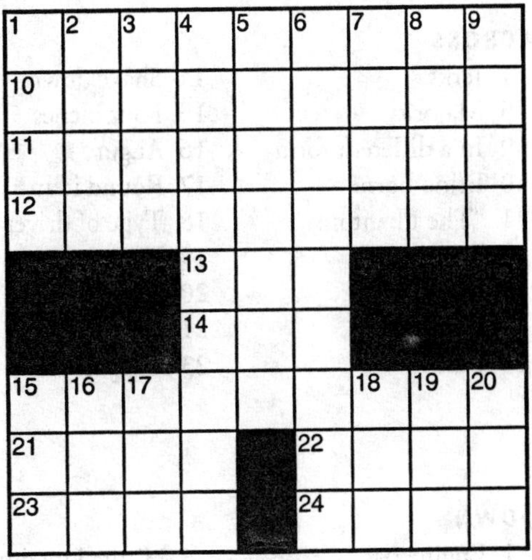
1
2
3
4
5
6
7
8
9
10
11
12
13
14
15
16
17
18
19
20
21
22
23
24

ACROSS

1 Jerks
5 Majority
9 In a different form
10 Brine-borne
11 "The Phantom Tollbooth" protagonist
12 Call
13 Can
14 Shake down
15 Four inches
16 Augury
17 Round items
18 Type of driver
19 Water white
20 Change, often
21 Debacle
23 Capped group

DOWN

1 Engine part
2 "I Married an Angel" scriptwriter
3 Draw
4 Foiled fellow
5 "Divisament dou Monde" subject
6 Hittite kingdom
7 Out
8 Sapience
22 ___ Erh (Lao-Tzu)

SOLUTIONS

PUZZLE 1

S	T	A	F	F		C	R	Y
P	I	P	E	R		A	Y	E
A	M	P	L	E		P	E	W
R	O	L	L	T	O	P		
K	N	E	E		F	I	T	S
		T	R	A	N	S	I	T
J	A	R		D	O	T	T	Y
O	W	E		A	T	O	L	L
B	E	E		M	E	L	E	E

PUZZLE 2

M	A	Z	E		L	I	M	B
O	X	E	N		E	D	I	E
B	E	N	T		T	A	X	I
			E	D		H	E	N
B	J	O	R	N	B	O	R	G
L	A	B		A	L			
O	P	E	C		U	T	A	H
C	A	S	H		T	O	M	E
K	N	E	E		O	N	Y	X

PUZZLE 3

	C	H	E	E	P	
	F	O	U	L	T	I	P
H	A	R	M		A	P	E	S
A	R	K	S		L	E	N	T
R	E					N	O
P	A	C	T		A	J	A	R
O	S	L	O		M	I	M	E
	T	A	D	P	O	L	E
	M	O	I	S	T

PUZZLE 4

S	U	R	E		F	U	J	I
C	H	E	W		A	F	A	R
R	U	L	E		C	O	R	K
E	R	A		H	E		
W	A	X	M	U	S	E	U	M
		I	T		R	N	A
M	A	R	X		S	O	C	K
A	L	O	U		I	D	L	E
D	E	E	P		P	E	E	R

PUZZLE 5

T	W	O		S	P	A	R	K
R	A	N		O	L	D	I	E
A	C	T		M	U	D	D	Y
S	K	A	T	E	R			
H	Y	P	E		A	S	E	A
			H	O	L	M	E	S
U	T	U	R	N		I	R	K
M	O	R	A	L		T	I	E
P	E	N	N	Y		H	E	W

PUZZLE 6

A	B	U	T		A	S	K	S
B	O	S	H		S	N	A	P
E	X	E	R	T		A	P	E
		D	A	R	T	G	U	N
A	T		S	A	O		T	D
M	R	C	H	I	P	S		
A	I	L		T	H	U	M	B
S	C	A	M		A	R	I	A
S	K	Y	E		T	E	X	T

PUZZLE 7

H	A	T	E		M	A	D	E
A	R	A	B		A	L	E	X
S	C	U	B	A	D	I	V	E
			G	A	B	O	R	
S	P	E	A	R	M	I	N	T
C	R	A	N	E				
R	O	T	T	E	N	E	G	G
A	M	I	S		A	W	R	Y
P	O	N	Y		P	E	R	M

PUZZLE 8

J	I	G		V	A	M	P
E	V	A		E	S	A	U
R	A	M	P		R	A	P	T
K	N	E	E	C	A	P	
		N	U	N			
	H	A	R	D	H	A	T
C	O	A	L		A	U	R	A
H	A	L	T		F	A	X
I	F	F	Y		F	B	I

PUZZLE 9

G	U	N		G	L	I	T	Z
A	S	I		R	O	M	E	O
B	A	N	J	O		P	A	R
	J	A	W			M	R	
S	N	A	G		P	E	S	O
H	I		T	U	X			
A	G	E		A	B	U	Z	Z
L	E	V	E	R		D	O	E
T	R	A	M	P		E	O	N

PUZZLE 10

	D	E	F	E	R		
	O	L	I	V	E		
M	I		A	X	E		F	A
E	D	E	N		S	P	A	R
E	A	R				A	T	E
T	H	A	W		S	P	A	N
S	O		A	P	T		L	A
	T	R	E	A	D		
	I	N	T	R	O		

PUZZLE 11

E	L	O	P	E		O	F	F
L	I	N	E	N		P	R	O
I	S		P	O	P	E	Y	E
Z	Z	Z		S	U	N		
A	T	O	M		B	U	L	B
	M	A	Y		P	A	R	
H	U	B	C	A	P		S	I
I	F	I		M	E	N	S	A
P	O	E		S	W	O	O	N

PUZZLE 12

A	D	S				A	C	E
R	O	T				H	O	E
C	H	E	C	K	B	O	O	K
			A	L	L	E	Y	
			M	O	U	N	T	
			P	A	T	C	H	
S	P	I	K	E	H	E	E	L
P	O	P				R	E	A
A	W	E				E	L	M

PUZZLE 13

```
G R A B B A G ■
R E L E A S E ■
A V I A N ■ L A M
V E E R S ■ G A
I N N S ■ C H E T
T U ■ F A U S T
Y E S ■ O P R A H
■ S C R O O G E
■ E V E N N O W
```

PUZZLE 14

```
I C E ■ ■ T E D
M A R E ■ A R L O
P R I M E T I M E
■ C E L L O ■
■ R A E ■
■ S A T A N ■
A P P L E S E E D
V O I D ■ T E R I
A P T ■ ■ D A M
```

PUZZLE 15

```
■ H A L ■
■ B O R I C ■
■ D U S T M O P
H E F T ■ A N E W
O F F ■ S K I
G O A D ■ R O O T
■ G L O B U L E
■ O Z O N E ■
■ E W E ■
```

PUZZLE 16

```
■ E G O ■
■ P R O N G ■
C A R E B E A R S
O U I ■ T I E
A D V ■ E V E
C I A ■ W E T
H O T P O T A T O
■ E L W A Y ■
■ Y E T ■
```

PUZZLE 17

B	R	O	W	■	A	T	O	M
L	E	A	H	■	P	E	A	R
T	A	K	E	A	P	A	R	T
■	■	■	A	L	L	■	■	■
■	■	■	T	O	E	■	■	■
■	■	■	G	U	T	■	■	■
L	I	N	E	D	R	I	V	E
O	D	O	R	■	E	V	E	N
W	O	R	M	■	E	Y	E	D

PUZZLE 18

E	L	K	■	■	J	A	M	B
B	O	I	L	■	A	R	E	A
B	U	D	A	B	B	O	T	T
■	■	M	Y	■	M	O	E	■
L	A	Z	E	■	L	A	O	S
A	W	E	■	S	O	■	■	■
B	A	B	Y	T	O	O	T	H
O	K	R	A	■	P	L	E	A
R	E	A	P	■	■	D	A	Y

PUZZLE 19

J	A	V	A	■	■	J	A	B
O	X	E	N	■	■	U	S	E
T	E	X	T	■	■	D	O	E
■	■	■	L	A	Y	O	F	F
■	■	■	E	W	E	■	■	■
B	A	R	R	E	L	■	■	■
E	R	A	■	■	L	I	Z	A
V	I	M	■	■	O	D	O	R
Y	A	P	■	■	W	O	O	F

PUZZLE 20

M	A	C	H	O	■	B	A	T
A	L	O	O	F	■	I	V	Y
N	E	W	T	■	■	Z	I	P
E	X	■	T	O	L	E	D	O
■	■	A	U	D	I	T	■	■
B	I	G	B	E	N	■	H	E
E	O	N	■	■	E	V	I	L
E	W	E	■	Q	U	I	R	K
P	A	W	■	S	P	I	T	E

PUZZLE 21

```
A C I D ■ ■ S T E M
J A N E ■ ■ H A Z E
A N N E ■ ■ ■ P R O
R E ■ J I G S A W
■ ■ ■ A C E ■ ■ ■
S A W Y E R ■ ■ B Y
I W O ■ ■ ■ B R I E
Z E R O ■ ■ I O T A
E D E N ■ ■ L E E R
```

PUZZLE 22

```
M A C A W ■ ■ O F F
E X U D E ■ ■ B O O
A L F ■ ■ ■ J O A N
L E F T F I E L D ■
■ ■ ■ A L L ■ ■ ■
F A N C Y T H A T
O H I O ■ ■ ■ A X E
R A N ■ P A R I S
M B A ■ A M I S S
```

PUZZLE 23

```
B B S ■ A C T ■
A L P ■ C O R A L
G U I D E L I N E
P E T E ■ T O T O
I N ■ ■ ■ E N
P O S T ■ V E R A
E S C A L A T O R
S E A M Y ■ C O D
■ ■ T E E ■ H M O
```

PUZZLE 24

```
D I S H ■ C H U M
O N C E ■ R E N O
C O R N S Y R U P
K N O C K ■ ■ M E
■ D E I C E ■
A H ■ ■ F L A S K
S O N O F A G U N
A S I A ■ M E M O
N E X T ■ P R O W
```

PUZZLE 25

A	Z	T	E	C		G	A	P
C	O	N	G	O		I	R	A
H	O	T	O	N		J	I	G
E	M			A	B	O	D	E
		P	U	R	E	E		
A	D	A	P	T			L	B
J	O	Y		I	N	D	I	A
A	P	T		S	E	U	S	S
R	E	V		T	W	E	A	K

PUZZLE 26

L	A	S	S			E	B	B
I	D	I	O	T		G	E	E
D	O	N	N	A		G	R	R
		G	I	N		B	Y	E
B	L	A	C	K	B	E	L	T
R	A	P		T	E	A		
I	T	O		O	N	T	A	P
A	I	R		P	E	E	V	E
N	N	E			T	R	A	P

PUZZLE 27

C	L	A	S	S	M	A	T	E
P	A	R	T	T	I	M	E	R
O	P	E	R	A	G	O	E	R
			N	A	G			
		T	W	E	R	P		
			N	A	H			
P	I	A	Z	A	D	O	R	A
A	L	M	A	M	A	T	E	R
P	E	P	P	E	R	O	N	I

PUZZLE 28

F	I	B		P	S	H	A	W
I	R	E		A	L	O	H	A
J	O	N		R	E	P	A	Y
I	N	J	O	K	E			
	S	I	D		P	J	S	
		D	R	Y	I	C	E	
S	O	N	J	A		F	U	R
A	D	H	O	C		F	B	I
W	E	L	B	Y		Y	A	K

206

PUZZLE 29

K	E	G	S		B	A	E	Z
A	C	R	E		O	G	L	E
F	L	A	T	B	R	O	K	E
K	A	Y		R	I	G		
A	T		H	E	S		M	A
	M	A	C		F	A	N	
S	P	A	R	K	P	L	U	G
O	O	Z	E		E	A	V	E
D	E	E	M		A	B	E	L

PUZZLE 30

	A	W	O	K	E	
	A	T	A	N	E	N	D
A	G	O	G		W	O	R	M
C	O	P			S	E	A
U	N				I	N
T	I	E			S	S	E
E	Z	R	A		C	H	E	T
	E	M	P	E	R	O	R
	A	R	N	I	E	

PUZZLE 31

M	O	B	Y		M	A	R	K
A	B	L	E		O	V	E	N
Z	E	U	S		M	I	N	E
E	Y	E	S	H	A	D	O	W
			I	O	N			
S	A	C	R	E	D	C	O	W
A	J	A	R		P	U	M	A
G	A	L	E		O	R	A	L
A	X	L	E		P	E	R	K

PUZZLE 32

E	C	O			C	O	A	T
A	R	K		M	A	P	L	E
S	E	A		A	L	I	A	S
Y	A	Y		E	V	E	N	T
R	M		O	W	E		A	D
I	S	S	U	E		O	R	R
D	O	W	N	S		S	K	I
E	D	I	C	T		L	I	V
R	A	G	E		O	N	E

PUZZLE 33

A	B	C	■	S	C	A	R	F
Z	O	O	■	H	O	V	E	R
T	W	O	■	W	A	V	Y	■
E	E	K	■	A	L	■	■	■
C	R	E	A	M	S	O	D	A
■	■	B	Y	■	Z	A	P	■
L	I	M	B	■	Z	I	P	■
A	R	R	O	W	■	I	L	L
B	E	T	T	E	■	E	Y	E

PUZZLE 34

H	O	M	E	A	L	O	N	E
A	S	I	A	M	I	N	O	R
B	A	L	T	I	M	O	R	E
I	K	E	■	S	O	■	■	■
T	A	R	A	■	S	U	M	S
■	■	T	I	■	N	A	P	■
P	A	V	A	R	O	T	T	I
A	P	H	R	O	D	I	T	E
Y	E	S	I	N	D	E	E	D

PUZZLE 35

R	E	S	C	I	N	D	■
A	V	I	A	T	I	O	N
T	E	X	M	E	X	■	E	D
■	G	E	M	■	C	I	A
G	A	U	L	■	M	O	L	D
U	R	N	■	J	I	B	■
M	A	■	B	A	C	A	L	L
■	B	O	O	G	A	L	O	O
■	W	A	S	H	T	U	B

PUZZLE 36

■	■	P	R	I	C	E	S	■
E	R	I	E	C	A	N	A	L
W	O	L	V	E	R	I	N	E
E	Y	E	■	H	E	D	G	E
■	■	■	B	O	W	■	■	■
M	I	M	I	C	■	I	R	A
B	R	E	A	K	E	V	E	N
A	I	S	L	E	S	E	A	T
■	S	A	Y	Y	E	S	■

208

PUZZLE 37

A	P	R			H	A	L	F
S	A	O		H	I	R	E	D
E	B	B		O	T	T	E	R
A	L	I		D	U	D		
	O	N	P	A	P	E	R	
	H	A	D			A	H	A
S	W	O	R	D		L	I	P
K	O	O	K	Y		E	N	E
Y	O	D	A			R	E	X

PUZZLE 38

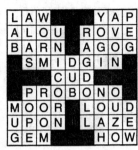

L	A	W			Y	A	P
A	L	O	U		R	O	V	E
B	A	R	N		A	G	O	G
	S	M	I	D	G	I	N	
		C	U	D			
	P	R	O	B	O	N	O	
M	O	O	R		L	O	U	D
U	P	O	N		L	A	Z	E
G	E	M			H	O	W	

PUZZLE 39

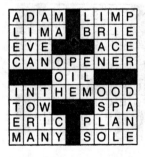

A	D	A	M		L	I	M	P
L	I	M	A		B	R	I	E
E	V	E			A	C	E	
C	A	N	O	P	E	N	E	R
		O	I	L			
I	N	T	H	E	M	O	O	D
T	O	W			S	P	A	
E	R	I	C		P	L	A	N
M	A	N	Y		S	O	L	E

PUZZLE 40

D	A	Z	E	D		S	K	I
A	R	O	M	A		T	I	N
F	L	O	P		M	O	C	K
T	O	M	A	H	A	W	K	
			T	A	C			
	S	C	H	M	A	L	T	Z
C	A	R	Y		B	A	S	E
U	F	O		F	R	I	A	R
P	E	W		M	E	T	R	O

209

PUZZLE 41

B	A	R	B			S	A	M
A	L	O	U			P	L	Y
R	E	E	F		Q	U	I	T
D	C		F	O	U	R	T	H
		C	A	B	I	N		
P	R	O	L	I	X		V	S
L	O	C	O		O	M	I	T
O	A	K			T	U	N	A
P	R	Y			E	D	E	N

PUZZLE 42

C	H	I	R	P		A	M	P
A	U	D	I	O		L	O	U
P	R	O	N	G		A	L	P
			S	O		M	A	P
L	O	V	E	S	T	O	R	Y
U	F	O			T	I		
C	U	D			I	T	E	M	S
A	S	K		C	H	E	E	K
S	E	A		K	E	L	L	Y

PUZZLE 43

A	Q	U	A			P	J	S
P	U	T	T	Y		L	O	U
T	I	A	R	A		A	C	E
		T	H	E	K	I	N	K	S
			S	U	N			
F	A	S	T	T	A	L	K	
I	N	K		S	W	I	N	E
S	K	I		K	A	Z	O	O
H	A	M		Y	A	W	N	

PUZZLE 44

	R	A	S	C	A	L	
	E	L	P	A	S	O	
	S	O	U	R	P	U	S	S
S	H	O	R	T			C	O
T	A	F	T		C	L	A	M
U	P			C	R	A	N	E
D	E	C	K	H	A	N	D	
		P	I	A	Z	Z	A	
		U	N	R	E	A	L	

PUZZLE 45

F	I	B				P	J	S
U	R	I	A	H	H	E	E	P
N	E	D	B	E	A	T	T	Y
			S	L	Y			
			T	I	S			
			A	P	E			
M	E	D	I	A	E	V	A	L
B	L	I	N	D	D	A	T	E
A	M	P				T	E	X

PUZZLE 46

B	B						F	F
O	O	P				T	A	O
B	O	U	T		J	U	M	P
	P	R	O	P	A	N	E	
		P	O	I	S	E		
	G	O	N	E	O	F	F	
M	U	S	S		N	U	L	L
A	L	E				L	E	O
P	P					X	X

PUZZLE 47

H	O	M	E	M	A	K	E	R
U	N	A	N	I	M	I	T	Y
R	A	I	N	D	A	N	C	E
			D	U	D			
			I	L	K			
			E	I	S			
D	R	E	A	M	L	A	N	D
O	I	L	T	A	N	K	E	R
I	M	M	E	N	S	I	T	Y

PUZZLE 48

B	E	D		F	L	A	K	Y
O	W	E		L	O	R	N	E
Z	E	L	D	A		K	E	N
		L	O	S			L	T
B	E	A	C	H	B	A	L	L
U	M			C	U	B		
N	I	P		U	S	U	R	P
C	L	I	M	B		Z	O	O
H	E	N	C	E		Z	E	E

211

PUZZLE 49

```
C L A I M ▮ M T V
H O N D A ▮ E W E
A R T Y ▮ K N O X
I R E L A N D ▮ ▮
M E ▮ L I E ▮ M I
▮ ▮ F I R E M A N
E P I C ▮ C A L L
B I N ▮ M A P L E
B E D ▮ U P S E T
```

PUZZLE 50

```
A B E ▮ ▮ ▮ C A P
C A D E T ▮ I R E
T I N G E ▮ A L E
S T A G E D O O R
▮ ▮ ▮ O D E ▮ ▮ ▮
J O A N O F A R C
E B B ▮ F E V E R
R O B ▮ F R O D O
K E Y ▮ ▮ ▮ W O W
```

PUZZLE 51

```
T A M P A ▮ D U B
A W A I T ▮ R H O
B L O C ▮ ▮ U S
▮ ▮ N A B O R S
E L A I N E M A Y
T O U C A N ▮ ▮ ▮
H O ▮ ▮ H E L P
A S S ▮ J U L I A
N E T ▮ A R M E D
```

PUZZLE 52

```
F U M E ▮ B A L E
A R I D ▮ R E E K
T I C ▮ A G O G
E A R ▮ E W E ▮
S H O T G L A S S
▮ W A G ▮ N I L
A J A X ▮ S T U
D O V E ▮ F E A R
D E E D ▮ E A R P
```

PUZZLE 53

```
F I E L D G O A L
I N F E R E N C E
B A L T I M O R E
■ ■ A S P ■ ■ I D
W I T ■ ■ C D S ■
O R ■ ■ I S H ■ ■
F E E D S T O R E
A N N A P U R N A
T E D D Y B E A R
```

PUZZLE 54

```
C H A F F ■ F B I
R U M O R ■ L A M
A D O R E ■ A M P
I S S U E ■ P B ■
G O ■ M A C ■ O P
■ N D ■ G O G O L
O B I ■ E L I Z A
D A M ■ N O B L Y
D Y E ■ T R E E S
```

PUZZLE 55

```
E L F ■ ■ S P E W
B E A ■ S T A R E
B E T ■ T I T L E
■ ■ C R A F T E D
■ H I L L Y ■
C R A N K E D ■
R A N G E ■ U S A
A R C E D ■ K I D
B E E R ■ E N D
```

PUZZLE 56

```
■ ■ ■ B O W ■ ■ ■
■ ■ ■ A P E ■ ■ ■
■ ■ ■ R E S ■ ■ ■
U P P E R C A S E
M I A F A R R O W
P A L A T A B L E
■ ■ ■ C I V ■ ■ ■
■ ■ ■ E V E ■ ■ ■
■ ■ ■ D E N ■ ■ ■
```

PUZZLE 57

M	O	H	A	W	K		S	T
A	R	E	T	H	A		H	O
P	I	P	E	O	R	G	A	N
			L	E	A	V	E	
S	C	A	V	E	N	G	E	R
M	A	R	I	N				
A	S	T	R	O	T	U	R	F
R	E		U	T	O	P	I	A
T	Y		S	E	N	S	O	R

PUZZLE 58

H	A	S		D	R	A	M	A
A	N	T		R	O	V	E	R
Z	E	E		A	B	A	S	E
E	W	E		G	O		H	A
	P	H	O	T	O			
I	S		A	N		O	L	E
D	W	A	R	F		M	I	X
L	A	P	E	L		P	E	A
E	N	E	M	Y		H	U	M

PUZZLE 59

C	R	Y			J	A	P	E
Z	O	O		C	O	B	R	A
A	S	K		A	B	B	O	T
R	Y	E	B	R	E	A	D	
		A	P	T				
	Z	E	R	O	H	O	U	R
Z	O	R	R	O		C	H	I
A	N	G	E	L		H	O	P
P	E	O	N			S	H	E

PUZZLE 60

I	R	A		B	A	T	O	N
D	E	S	D	E	M	O	N	A
A	S	H	E		B	L	O	B
H	E				L	E		
O	T	I	S		E	T	C	H
	M	E					R	E
P	A	P	A		Y	V	E	S
E	D	E	L	W	E	I	S	S
P	O	I	S	E		A	T	E

214

PUZZLE 61

PUZZLE 62

F	O	C	I			S	T	U	B
I	R	O	N			H	O	B	O
B	R	U	S	H	U	P	O	N	
		N	O	S	E	B	A	G	

(Puzzle 61 and 62 shown as completed crossword grids)

PUZZLE 63

PUZZLE 64

215

PUZZLE 65

PUZZLE 66

PUZZLE 67

PUZZLE 68

PUZZLE 69

PUZZLE 70

L	I	S	P			P	L	O	P
I	R	M	A			L	A	N	A
L	I	O	N	T	A	M	E	R	
A	S	K		A	Z				
C	H	E	W	B	A	C	C	A	
			O	B		A	L	P	
B	E	L	L	Y	F	L	O	P	
A	S	O	F			O	V	A	L
G	E	N	E			P	E	K	E

PUZZLE 71

B	I	G	D	I	P	P	E	R
A	V	A	I	L	A	B	L	E
C	O	P	I	O	U	S	L	Y
O	R	E		V	S			
N	Y		F	E	E		G	A
		A	L			L	O	G
H	A	M	M	U	R	A	B	I
E	R	I	E	C	A	N	A	L
R	E	A	D	Y	M	A	D	E

PUZZLE 72

217

PUZZLE 73

PUZZLE 74

PUZZLE 75

PUZZLE 76

PUZZLE 77

	S	C	A	B		I	D	O
	G	O	G	O		N	I	N
	T	R	I	O		T	N	T
	F	I	N	K		E	G	O
D	R	A	G	S	T	R	I	P
R	I	N		H	Y	M	N	
A	D	D		E	P	E	E	
M	A	E		L	E	N	S	
S	Y	R		F	A	T	S	

PUZZLE 78

J	O	E	L	C	A	I	R	O
A	N	G	E	L	F	O	O	D
M	A	G	N	I	T	U	D	E
			A	P	E			
J	O	S	H		R	E	B	A
A	S	T	O		M	E	A	L
P	A	R	R		A	R	N	O
A	K	I	N		T	I	F	F
N	A	P	E		H	E	F	T

PUZZLE 79

			C	O	M	M	A
	F	I	S	H	H	O	O	K
	E	T	H	I	O	P	I	A
	S	C	A	N				
	S	H	Y	A	W	A	Y	
				T	O	G	A	
R	E	D	R	O	V	E	R	
I	R	O	N	W	E	E	D	
B	R	I	A	N				

PUZZLE 80

J	E	S	T		R	O	M	P
O	V	E	R		E	V	I	L
B	E	A	U		L	A	M	A
			E	T	A	L	I	I
L	P		F	A	Y		C	D
A	A	F	A	I	R			
L	U	L	L		A	F	A	R
A	L	A	S		C	O	L	A
W	A	K	E		E	X	I	T

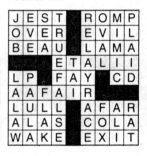

PUZZLE 81

```
H A L L O ■ K I T
A B O U T ■ A M Y
D E A T H T R A P
■ ■ T E E N A G E
B A H ■ ■ T E E
A S S U A G E ■ ■
T W O S H A K E S
H A M ■ E M I L E
E N E ■ M E D I A
```

PUZZLE 82

```
■ ■ P O S E A S
■ ■ E N I G M A
■ ■ S U N G O D
A N T S ■ N E E
Z O O ■ C O B ■
H A M ■ O L G A ■
E L A I N E ■ ■
R E A D E R ■ ■
D A M A S K ■ ■
```

PUZZLE 83

```
M I L K ■ T A P
A L O G ■ H U H
C L U B S O D A
■ ■ K R I S ■
■ A L D E N T E
M A R E ■ ■ ■
P L A T Y P U S
L A P ■ E A S E
E W E ■ A P E X
```

PUZZLE 84

```
M R T ■ F A D
I O U ■ A T E
N A T A S H A
E R U P T E D
■ ■ P T A ■
B A R R A C K
O R A T I O N
D E C ■ D U O
E L K ■ A P T
```

PUZZLE 85

L	E	S	S	E	N	
A	L	T	M	A	N	
U	P	R	I	S	E	
D	A	I	L	Y		I	S	M
E	S	P	E	R	A	N	T	O
R	O	E		I	N	N	E	R
		I	D	E	A	L	S
		G	E	N	T	L	E
		O	R	D	E	A	L

PUZZLE 86

		P	I	A	N	O	S
		B	A	D	D	E	B	T
	M	A	N	E	A	T	E	R
F	A	N		A	M	P	L	E
I	R	K	S		E	R	I	E
A	S	C	A	P		I	S	T
S	H	A	M	R	O	C	K
C	A	R	B	I	N	E
O	L	D	A	G	E

PUZZLE 87

		T	R	I	C	I	A
		C	O	O	L	A	N	T
E	P	H	E	M	E	R	A	L
A	R	I	D		D	O	R	E
R	A	N			L	A	A
F	L	A	T		P	I	G	S
L	I	S	A	B	O	N	E	T
A	N	E	M	O	N	E
P	E	A	P	O	D

PUZZLE 88

		W	A	S	H	E	S
		A	M	P	E	R	E
		C	M	A	J	O	R
S	A	M	S	O	N	I	T	E
A	P	E				R	I	N
P	O	K	E	R	F	A	C	E
P	L	O	V	E	R	
E	L	N	I	N	O	
D	O	G	L	E	G	

PUZZLE 89

A	J	A	R		M	A	S	T
B	A	L	E		E	D	N	A
E	V	E	N		L	A	I	R
T	A	X	E	X	E	M	P	T
		H	E	X	E	S		
A	V	A				M	O	P
L	O	L	L		W	I	D	E
P	L	E	A		O	T	I	S
S	T	Y	X		W	H	E	T

PUZZLE 90

O	F						V	A
O	R						I	N
M	E	L	G	I	B	S	O	N
	D	O	A	D	E	A	L	
	E	N	F	O	R	C	E	
	R	E	F	L	E	C	T	
F	I	R	E	S	T	O	R	M
A	C						E	D
O	K						D	I

PUZZLE 91

A	R	T	I	C	H	O	K	E
C	O	O	N	H	O	U	N	D
L	O	U	G	E	H	R	I	G
U	M	S		R	U	S	T	Y
			A	R	M			
B	R	A	D	Y		A	V	A
A	U	T	O	P	I	L	O	T
I	N	T	R	I	C	A	T	E
T	E	N	N	E	S	S	E	E

PUZZLE 92

S	P	R	I	N	G	Y		
T	R	E	M	O	L	O		
R	O	S	A		I	R	M	A
A	P	T		S	T	E	E	L
T	O		B	I	Z		A	R
U	S	H	E	R		N	N	E
M	E	A	L		A	I	D	A
		F	L	A	N	K	E	D
		T	A	N	N	E	R	Y

222

PUZZLE 93

```
    S P I R E D
    O R M O L U
    D O M A I N
  S A V O R
  A W I D E
  F A D E D
A B A T E S
P A R E N T
T H I R T Y
```

PUZZLE 94

```
C R O S S W O R D
L O N C H A N E Y
A B O R I G I N E
P E R I M E T E R
      P M S
      T E L
A S S U R A N C E
S P U R   V E I L
H Y P E   E D A M
```

PUZZLE 95

```
C A D S   M A S S
A N E W   A S E A
M I L O   R I N G
S T I R   C A S E
H A N D   O M E N
A L E S   P I L E
F O A M   O N E S
T O T A L L O S S
  S E N I O R S
```